PENPALS
for
Handwriting

Foundation 1 Teacher's Book and CD

(3–5 years)

Gill Budgell   Kate Ruttle

Series Consultants
Sue Palmer   Dr Rhona Stainthorp

Contents

CAMBRIDGE   HITACHI

www.cambridge-hitachi.com

Scope and sequence

Foundation 1/3–5 years

DEVELOPING GROSS MOTOR SKILLS
1 The vocabulary of movement
2 Large movements
3 Responding to music

DEVELOPING FINE MOTOR SKILLS
4 Hand and finger play
5 Making and modelling
6 Links to art
7 Using one-handed tools and equipment

DEVELOPING PATTERNS AND BASIC LETTER MOVEMENTS
8 Pattern-making
9 Responding to music
10 Investigating straight line patterns
11 Investigating loops
12 Investigating circles
13 Investigating angled patterns
14 Investigating eights and spirals

Foundation 2/Primary 1

Term 2
1 Introducing long ladder letters: *l, i, t, u, j, y*
2 Practising long ladder letters: *l, i*
3 Practising long ladder letters: *t, u*
4 Practising long ladder letters: *j, y*
5 Practising all the long ladder letters
6 Introducing one-armed robot letters: *r, b, n, h, m, k, p*
7 Practising one-armed robot letters: *b, n*
8 Practising one-armed robot letters: *h, m*
9 Practising one-armed robot letters: *k, p*
10 Practising all the one-armed robot letters
11 Introducing capitals for one-armed robot letters: *R, B, N, H, M, K, P*
12 Introducing capitals for long ladder letters: *L, I, T, U, J, Y*

Term 3
13 Introducing curly caterpillar letters: *c, a, d, o, s, g, q, e, f*
14 Practising curly caterpillar letters: *a, d*
15 Practising curly caterpillar letters: *o, s*
16 Practising curly caterpillar letters: *g, q*
17 Practising curly caterpillar letters: *e, f*
18 Practising all the curly caterpillar letters
19 Introducing zig-zag monster letters: *z, v, w, x*
20 Practising zig-zag monster letters: *v, w, x*
21 Introducing capitals for curly caterpillar letters: *C, A, D, O, S, G, Q, E, F*
22 Introducing capitals for zig-zag monster letters: *Z, V, W, X*
23 Exploring *ch, th* and *sh*

Year 1/Primary 2

Term 1
1 Letter formation practice: long ladder family
2 Letter formation practice: one-armed robot family
3 Letter formation practice: curly caterpillar family
4 Letter formation practice: zig-zag monster family
5 Practising the vowels: *i*
6 Practising the vowels: *u*
7 Practising the vowels: *a*
8 Practising the vowels: *o*
9 Practising the vowels: *e*
10 Letter formation practice: capital letters

Term 2
11 Introducing diagonal join to ascender: joining *at, all*
12 Practising diagonal join to ascender: joining *th*
13 Practising diagonal join to ascender: joining *ch*
14 Practising diagonal join to ascender: joining *cl*
15 Introducing diagonal join, no ascender: joining *in, im*
16 Practising diagonal join, no ascender: joining *cr, tr, dr*
17 Practising diagonal join, no ascender: joining *lp, mp*
18 Introducing diagonal join, no ascender, to an anticlockwise letter: joining *id, ig*
19 Practising diagonal join, no ascender, to an anticlockwise letter: joining *nd, ld*
20 Practising diagonal join, no ascender, to an anticlockwise letter: joining *ng*

Term 3
21 Practising diagonal join, no ascender: joining *ee*
22 Practising diagonal join, no ascender: joining *ai, ay*
23 Practising diagonal join, no ascender: joining *ime, ine*
24 Introducing horizontal join, no ascender: joining *op, oy*
25 Practising horizontal join, no ascender: joining *one, ome*
26 Introducing horizontal join, no ascender, to an anticlockwise letter: joining *oa, og*
27 Practising horizontal join, no ascender, to an anticlockwise letter: joining *wa, wo*
28 Introducing horizontal join to ascender: joining *ol, ot*
29 Practising horizontal join to ascender: joining *wh, oh*
30 Introducing horizontal and diagonal joins to ascender, to an anticlockwise letter: joining *of, if*
31 Assessment

Year 2/Primary 3

Term 1
1 How to join in a word: high-frequency words
2 Introducing the break letters: *j, g, x, y, z, b, f, p, q, r, s*
3 Practising diagonal join to ascender in words: *eel, eet*
4 Practising diagonal join, no ascender, in words: *a_e*
5 Practising diagonal join, no ascender, to an anticlockwise letter in words: *ice, ide*
6 Practising horizontal join, no ascender, in words: *ow, ou*
7 Practising horizontal join, no ascender, in words: *oy, oi*
8 Practising horizontal join, no ascender, to an anticlockwise letter in words: *oa, ode*
9 Practising horizontal join to ascender in words: *ole, obe*
10 Practising horizontal join to ascender in words: *ook, ool*

Term 2
11 Practising diagonal join to r: *ir, ur, er*
12 Practising horizontal join to r: *or, oor*
13 Introducing horizontal join from r to ascender: *url, irl, irt*
14 Introducing horizontal join from r: *ere*
15 Practising joining to and from r: *air*
16 Introducing diagonal join to s: *dis*
17 Introducing horizontal join to s: *ws*
18 Introducing diagonal join from s to ascender: *sh*
19 Introducing diagonal join from s, no ascender: *si, su, se, sp, sm*
20 Introducing horizontal join from r to an anticlockwise letter: *rs*

Term 3
21 Practising diagonal join to an anticlockwise letter: *ea, ear*
22 Introducing horizontal join to and from f to ascender: *ft, fl*
23 Introducing horizontal join from f, no ascender: *fu, fr*
24 Introducing *qu* (diagonal join, no ascender)
25 Introducing *rr* (horizontal join, no ascender)
26 Introducing *ss* (diagonal join, no ascender, to an anticlockwise letter)
27 Introducing *ff* (horizontal join to ascender)
28 Capital letter practice: height of ascenders and capitals
29 Assessment
30 Assessment

Scope and sequence

Year 3 / Primary 4

Term 1
1 Revising joins in a word: long vowel phonemes
2 Revising joins in a word: *le*
3 Revising joins in a word: *ing*
4 Revising joins in a word: high-frequency words
5 Revising joins in a word: new vocabulary
6 Revising joins in a word: *un*, *de*
7 Revising joins to and from s: *dis*
8 Revising joins to and from r: *re*, *pre*
9 Revising joins to and from f: *ff*
10 Revising joins: *qu*

Term 2
11 Introducing joining b and p: diagonal join, no ascender, *bi*, *bu*, *pi*, *pu*
12 Practising joining b and p: diagonal join, no ascender, to an anticlockwise letter, *ba*, *bo*, *pa*, *po*
13 Practising joining b and p: diagonal join to ascender, *bl*, *ph*
14 Relative sizes of letters: silent letters
15 Parallel ascenders: high-frequency words
16 Parallel descenders: adding *y* to words
17 Relative size and consistency: *ly*, *less*, *ful*
18 Relative size and consistency: capitals
19 Speed and fluency practice: *er*, *est*
20 Speed and fluency practice: opposites

Term 3
21 Consistency in spacing: *mis*, *anti*, *ex*
22 Consistency in spacing: *non*, *co*
23 Consistency in spacing: apostrophes
24 Layout, speed and fluency practice: address
25 Layout, speed and fluency practice: dialogue
26 Layout, speed and fluency practice: poem
27 Layout speed and fluency practice: letter
28 Handwriting style: calligrams
29 Assessment
30 Handwriting style: acrostics

Year 4 / Primary 5

Term 1
1 Revising joins in a word: *ness*, *ship*
2 Revising joins in a word: *ing*, *ed*
3 Revising joins in a word: *s*
4 Revising joins in a word: *ify*
5 Revising joins in a word: *nn*, *mm*, *ss*
6 Revising parallel ascenders: *tt*, *ll*, *bb*
7 Revising parallel ascenders and descenders: *pp*, *ff*
8 Revising joins to an anticlockwise letter: *cc*, *dd*
9 Revising break letters: alphabetical order
10 Linking spelling and handwriting: related words

Term 2
11 Introducing sloped writing
12 Parallel ascenders: *al*, *ad*, *af*
13 Parallel descenders and break letters: *ight*, *ough*
14 Size, proportion and spacing: *ious*
15 Size, proportion and spacing: *able*, *ful*
16 Size, proportion and spacing: *fs*, *ves*
17 Speed and fluency: abbreviations for notes
18 Speed and fluency: notemaking
19 Speed and fluency: drafting
20 Speed and fluency: lists

Term 3
21 Size, proportion and spacing: *v*, *k*
22 Size, proportion and spacing: *ic*, *ist*
23 Size, proportion and spacing: *ion*
24 Size, proportion and spacing: *its*, *it's*
25 Speed and fluency: *ible*, *able*
26 Speed and fluency: diminutives
27 Print alphabet: captions, headings, labels
28 Print capitals: posters
29 Assessment
30 Presentational skills: font styles

Years 5 & 6 / Primary 6 & 7

Basics
1 Letter formation: *l* family
2 Letter formation: *r* family
3 Letter formation: *c* family
4 Letter formation: *z* family
5 Letter formation: *L* family
6 Letter formation: *R* family
7 Letter formation: *C* family
8 Letter formation: *Z* family
9 Letter formation at speed
10 Number formation
11 Joining: diagonal joins
12 Joining: horizontal joins
13 Joining: tricky joins
14 Joining at speed
15 Style at speed: variations on *f*, *g*, *s*, *t*, *y*
16 Style at speed: variations on *j*, *v*, *w*, *x*, *z*
17 Letter size: consistency of lower case letters
18 Letter size: comparison of lower case letters
19 Letter size: lower case letters and capital letters
20 Letter orientation: writing letters on the baseline
21 Letter orientation: ascenders and descenders
22 Spacing: between letters
23 Spacing: between words
24 Parallels: upright ascenders and descenders
25 Parallels: sloping ascenders and descenders
26 Self-assessment: handwriting check-list

Presentation
27 Writing for different purposes
28 Lettering styles: capital letters
29 Labelling: print alphabet
30 Labelling: diagrams
31 Pattern making: geometric patterns
32 Pattern making: symbols and maps

Penpals rationale

Even in this technological, computer-literate age, good handwriting remains fundamental to our children's educational achievement. *Penpals for Handwriting* is the only handwriting programme to offer a progression from 3 to 11 years and will help you teach children to develop fast, fluent, legible handwriting.

Penpals ensures that appropriate Early Years experiences are offered before more formal teaching begins.

Traditional principles in the contemporary classroom

We believe that:

1   A flexible, fluent and legible handwriting style empowers children to write with confidence and creativity. This is an entitlement that needs careful progression and skilful teaching.

2   Handwriting is a developmental process with its own distinctive stages of sequential growth. We have identified five stages that form the basic organisational structure of *Penpals*:
1.   Readiness for handwriting; gross and fine motor skills leading to pattern and letter formation (Foundation, 3–5 years)
2.   Beginning to join (Key Stage 1, 5–7 years)
3.   Securing the joins (Key Stage 1 and lower Key Stage 2, 5–9 years)
4.   Practising speed and fluency (Key Stage 2, 7–9 years)
5.   Presentational skills (upper Key Stage 2, 9–11 years)

3   Handwriting must be actively taught: this can be done when appropriate in association with phonics and spelling. Learning to associate the kinaesthetic handwriting movement with the visual letter pattern and the aural phonemes will help children with learning to spell.

A practical approach

Penpals offers a practical approach to support the delivery of handwriting teaching in the context of the modern curriculum. At Foundation 1 (3–5 years) this means support with:

- **Time** A series of units offer time-saving, practical and fun ideas for ensuring the systematic practice of handwriting skills. Most of the ideas are generic and can easily be adapted to the current topic or theme in the class.
- **Planning** *Penpals* helps with long-, medium- and short-term planning and is correlated to national guidelines.
- **Practice** *Penpals* offers a wealth of opportunities for practising skills in imaginative situations and also provides 'ideas templates' (A4 and A5) which may be copied, enlarged or adapted.
- **Revision** *Penpals* offers 'readiness for handwriting' assessment checks as well as teacher–child shared record-keeping opportunities.
- **Motivation** The *Penpals* materials are written with the support of children, nursery nurses, classroom assistants, teachers, foundation consultants and handwriting experts to stimulate and motivate young children as learners.
- **ICT** Use the *Penpals* audio CD and the *Penpals CD-ROMs* to enrich and extend children's early handwriting experiences.

Penpals: Foundation 1 can also be used to support children with special needs.

A few words from the experts…

Sue Palmer (literacy specialist and educational writer)

Handwriting has often been the 'Cinderella-skill' in terms of the teaching of writing and too many published resources have relied far too much (and too soon) on worksheet materials. For many young children, worksheets in Nursery and Reception classes can often be counterproductive. Instead, we should be linking preparation for handwriting to music, movement and art, and ensuring that these experiences are both appropriate for handwriting and enjoyable for the children. In this respect, the practical suggestions in the Teacher's Book and CD of *Penpals: Foundation 1* are the best materials I have ever come across.

Catherine Elsey (State Registered Occupational Therapist, National Handwriting Association)

Handwriting is the ultimate fine motor task, which additionally requires skills in eye-hand co-ordination, organisation and sequencing. We expect these skills of very young children, all too often before they are developmentally ready, for example requiring fine motor control of fingers before having postural stability. Pre-writing skills can be learnt by young children, but we should not expect letter and number formation until they can master an oblique cross (X), which requires crossing midline. Children with illegible handwriting or where writing causes discomfort have often picked up 'bad habits' when younger. Many children with handwriting difficulties are referred to Occupational Therapists who can help improve letter formation, fluency and pencil grip for example, but it would be of greater benefit to make sure children get the basics of handwriting correct at the outset. Penpals for Handwriting will help establish the right skills at the right time for each child and so make this essential communication tool a pleasure rather than a chore.

Links to national guidelines

Penpals Foundation 1 supports many national guidelines including:

- The Early Years Foundation Stage (EYFS 2007) incorporating *Curriculum Guidance for the Foundation Stage* (2000);
- *Foundation Stage Profile Handbook* (2003); Practitioners should continue to use the *Foundation Stage Profile* (FSP) handbook and booklet. From September 2008 it will become the *Early Years Foundation Stage Profile* (EYFSP).
- *Primary Frameworks for literacy and mathematics* (Primary National Strategy 2006);
- *Letters and sounds – Principles and Practice of High Quality Phonics* (DfES 2007);
- *Curriculum Framework for Children 3 to 5* (Scottish Consultative Council on the Curriculum);
- *Curricular Guidance for Pre-School Education* (Northern Ireland council for the Curriculum, Examinations and Assessment).

Following the key messages of best Early Years practice *Penpals* supports the development of:

- control of gross and fine movements;
- vocabulary for talking about patterns and letter formation;
- oral patter to support the formation of letters within their letter families;
- links between phonemes and letters;
- efficient pencil hold and good posture;
- control of pencil marks to form letters correctly, to prepare for joining;
- opportunities for exploring shape and movement across the curriculum and in the environment.

Using technology for developing handwriting skills

Throughout *Penpals*, technology is used to enhance the teaching and learning of handwriting. At F1, the opportunities available through technology are particularly rich and varied.

Using the audio CD

Penpals Foundation 1 includes an audio CD featuring a range of rhymes, action activities and different styles of music. These encourage the development of gross and fine motor skills and the production of key patterns and basic letter movements. A full list of the audio CD tracks is printed inside the front cover. Suggestions on how to use the audio CD are given in units 3, 4 and 9, on pages 22, 24 and 34.

Using the Foundation 1 CD-ROM

The *Penpals Foundation 1 CD-ROM* for the interactive whiteboard exploits the key strengths of the whiteboard to create new and exciting opportunities to develop skills for handwriting. There are nine units, each of which is linked to units in this *Penpals Foundation 1 Teacher's Book*. The nine units can be used with a whole class of children or just a small group. Although the beginning of each session is discussion-based and led by an Early Years Practitioner, there are also plenty of opportunities for your children to explore different patterns through exciting, interactive activities. The development through each unit follows the same progression:

Warm up videos: These are whole-body activities which can be used to warm up the body and mind ready for the handwriting session.

Talk about screens: Pictures, animations and short video clips provide opportunities to extend children's appreciation of shapes and patterns in the environment. These images provide opportunities for developing and enhancing speaking and listening skills.

Try activity screens: Interactive games challenge children to practise and develop movements and patterns which are specific to the unit.

Penpals pad: Children can practise movements and patterns using a variety of motivating and colourful techniques.

Gallery: Samples of children's work for comparison and assessment for learning activities. You can also save your own class's work into this area for discussion or just display!

Penpals Foundation 1 with Letters and Sounds

Penpals Foundation 1 is ideally suited to children working within Phases 1 and 2 of *Letters and Sounds*. It is important that, as with Phase 1 of *Letters and Sounds*, *Penpals Foundation 1* should continue to be used throughout the Foundation Stage as children will continue to benefit from the activities even after they have begun working with the *Penpals Foundation 2* resources.

Penpals for Handwriting: Foundation 1
Match to *Early Years Foundation Stage* and *Primary Framework for literacy and mathematics*

Following the key messages of best Early Years practice *Penpals Foundation 1* supports the following progression as specified in the **Early Years Foundation Stage** (2007) and the *Primary Framework for literacy and mathematics* (2006):

Communication, Language and Literacy: Handwriting	Development (the 'stepping stones'– numbered here for ease of reference)	Look, listen and note	Effective practice	Planning and resourcing
22–36 months	1a Begin to show some control in their use of tools and equipment.	Ways in which children begin to develop fine motor skills, for example, the way they use their fingers when trying to do up buttons, pull up a zip, pour a drink or use a watering can.	Encourage children to handle and manipulate a variety of media and implements, for example, clay, finger-paint, spoons, brushes and shells.	Vary the range of tools and equipment located with familiar activities, for example, put small scoops, rakes or sticks with the sand.
30–50 months	1b Use one-handed tools and equipment. 2a Draw lines and circles using gross motor movements. 2b Manipulate objects with increasing control.	The way children control equipment and materials. The marks children like to make.	Provide activities that give children the opportunity and motivation to practise manipulative skills, for example, cooking and playing instruments.	Provide opportunities for large shoulder movements, for example, swirling ribbons in the air, batting balls suspended on rope and painting. Encourage children to make shapes like circles and zig-zags in the air and in their play, for example, with sand and water and brushes.
40–60+ months	3a Begin to use anticlockwise movement and retrace vertical lines. 3b Begin to form recognisable letters. 4 **(by end of R) Use a pencil and hold it effectively to form recognisable letters, most of which are correctly formed.**	Children's dexterity in using a range of tools in their play and writing. Children's formation of recognisable letters.	Teach children to form letters correctly, for example, when they label their paintings. Encourage children to practise letter shapes as they paint, draw and record, and as they write, for example, their names, the names of their friends and family, or captions. Continue writing practice in imaginative contexts, joining some letters if appropriate, for example, at, it, on.	Provide a variety of writing tools and paper, indoors and outdoors. Give children practice in forming letters correctly, for example, labelling their work, making cards and writing notices. Provide opportunities to write meaningfully, for example, by placing notepads by phones or having appointment cards in the role-play doctor's surgery.

Penpals Foundation 1 supports many other Early Learning Goals as set out in the EYFS. It is assumed that links to ELGs such as those relating to self-esteem, confidence, behaviour and self-control along with many others of a more generic kind will also be developed in the course of using this material. However, the most significant links to other ELGs are shown on page 7.

The *Penpals Foundation 2* materials offer further practice in these aspects of handwriting, and work more formally towards using a pencil, holding it effectively to form recognisable letters most of which are correctly formed. It is envisaged that *Penpals Foundation 1* and *Foundation 2* are used throughout the Foundation stage and alongside the chosen resource for delivering the discrete daily phonic session.

Unit number and focus	Specific stepping stone link towards the handwriting ELG	Language for communication	Language for thinking	Linking sounds and letters	Writing	Shape, space and measures	Exploration and investigation	Design and making skills	Movement	Sense of space	Using equipment	Using tools and materials	Exploring media and materials	Music	Imagination	Responding to experiences and expressing and communicating ideas
Developing gross motor skills																
1 The vocabulary of movement	1a	✓							✓					✓	✓	✓
2 Large movements	1a, 1b, 2a, 2b, 3a	✓							✓	✓	✓					
3 Responding to music	1a, 1b, 2a, 2b, 3a	✓		✓		✓			✓	✓				✓	✓	✓
Developing fine motor skills																
4 Hand and finger play	1a, 2a, 3a	✓		✓					✓					✓	✓	
5 Making and modelling	1a, 1b, 2b, 3a	✓						✓				✓	✓	✓	✓	
6 Links to art	1a, 1b, 2a, 2b, 3a	✓	✓					✓				✓	✓	✓	✓	
7 Using one-handed tools and equipment	1a, 1b, 2b, 3a, 3b, 4	✓			✓							✓	✓	✓	✓	
Developing patterns and basic letter movements																
8 Pattern-making	1a, 1b, 2a, 2b, 3a, 3b, (4)	✓	✓			✓	✓									
9 Responding to music	1a, 1b, 2a, 2b, 3a, 3b, (4)	✓				✓			✓	✓				✓	✓	✓
10 Investigating straight line patterns	1a, 1b, 2a, 2b, 3a, 3b, (4)	✓	✓		✓	✓	✓		✓			✓	✓			
11 Investigating loops	1a, 1b, 2a, 2b, 3a, 3b, (4)	✓	✓		✓	✓	✓		✓			✓	✓			
12 Investigating circles	1a, 1b, 2a, 2b, 3a, 3b, (4)	✓	✓		✓	✓	✓		✓			✓	✓			
13 Investigating angled patterns	1a, 1b, 2a, 2b, 3a, 3b, (4)	✓	✓		✓	✓	✓		✓			✓	✓			
14 Investigating eights and spirals	1a, 1b, 2a, 2b, 3a, 3b, (4)	✓	✓		✓	✓	✓		✓			✓	✓			

Assessment

The aim of assessment should be to find out what a child knows, understands or can do. *Penpals* can help you to make professional, informed judgements about children's achievements, experiences and preferences in areas that are likely to affect their progress in handwriting. Suggestions for a variety of different assessment types and purposes are included in this book: some are records of experience or achievement for you to share with colleagues and parents; others are observational indicators which can contribute to your professional understanding of individual children's development. The most comprehensive record of what children can achieve will be in your day-to-day observations of them at 'work and play'.

The *Early Years Foundation Stage Profile* (EYFSP) reminds us of the end of Foundation target for handwriting within Communication, Language and Literacy.

5 The child's writing consists of recognisable letters. Holds a pencil and uses it effectively to form recognisable letters, most of which are correctly formed.

When assessing this criterion, the practitioner should observe the child while engaged in a writing activity, to establish that the child is holding a pencil effectively and that letters are generally correctly formed, for example by the use of anti-clockwise movement and the retracing of vertical lines when appropriate.

Record-keeping

The Photocopy Master on page 12 offers a pro forma record-keeping sheet for children. You can give them opportunities to make patterns involving straight lines, loops, circles and zig-zags, but the templates can also be adapted for other experiences. Photocopy a sheet, record the activity type (e.g. sand play, finger painting, construction toys) in each quadrant and date it. There is sufficient space for you to record a brief comment or for the

children to make patterns, or to colour in the quadrant.

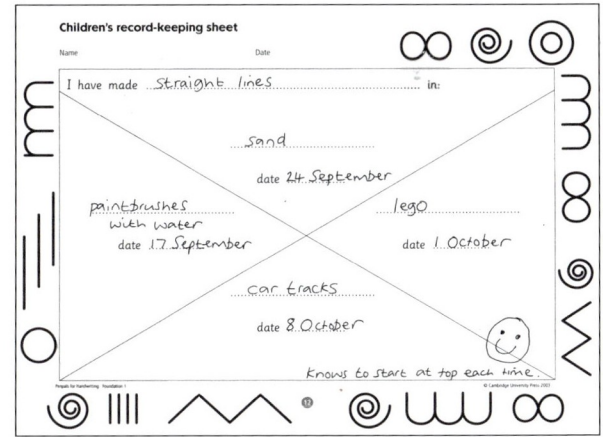

Handwriting pattern checklist

On page 11 there is a simple pattern-copying activity. Once children have acquired a good pencil hold and can sustain concentration for long enough to complete the activity, let them attempt to copy the patterns at the beginning of each term. This will give you evidence of progress as well as indicating which areas of pattern-making the children still need to practise.

The ideas templates in Units 8–14 can be photocopied, or alternatively they and the patterns around the units can be used to generate your own ideas for tracing or pattern-making activities. These can provide additional practice for handwriting patterns.

Cutting assessment

Page 10 can be photocopied for each child to demonstrate how well they can cut accurate lines. Date the assessment each time the children complete it and make a note of their dominant hand, scissor grip, etc.

Left-handed children often prefer to use scissors in a clockwise direction.

Ensuring readiness for handwriting

- **Hoop check** (see page 20) A PE session in which children are given time to play freely with hoops can be used to make assessments about how 'ready' for handwriting the children are.
- **Pencil hold** (see page 9) This sheet shows the general development of pencil holds and suggests approximate ages at which children progress from one stage to the next. These should be treated as guidelines only but, until children are able to hold a pencil with a relaxed grip and make finer finger movements, they are unlikely to be physically ready to begin formal letter formation activities.
- **Finger check** If children can touch their thumb to each of their fingers in turn, this is a good indicator that their fine motor skills are well developed enough for them to begin handwriting.

Right- or left-handed?

Many of the *Penpals* warm-up activities, pattern explorations and movement pictures encourage children to experiment using both the left and right hand, sometimes simultaneously. This is to stimulate the co-ordination of body action and brain.

Many young children do not determine their dominant hand until they are in the Foundation stage at nursery or school. It is important to make left-handed scissors available while children are exploring laterality. Once children have decided which is their dominant hand, try to avoid elbows bumping by ensuring that left-handed children do not work too closely to the right of right-handed children.

Developmental levels of pencil hold

*Ages are approximate

1–2 years

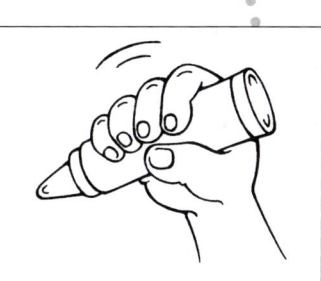

- Held with fisted hand.
- Arm moves as a unit.

2–3 years

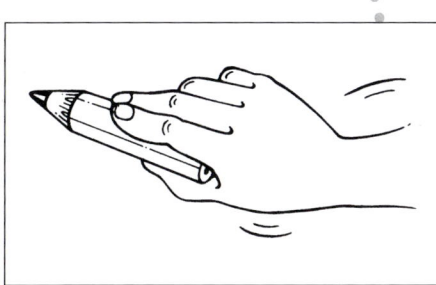

- Held with fingers.
- Forearm moves as a unit.

3–4 years

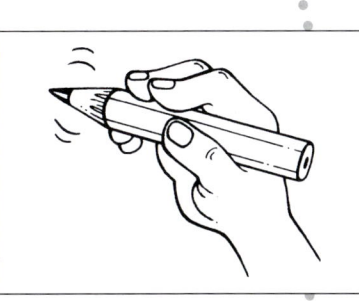

- Held with crude approximation of thumb, index and middle fingers.
- Hand moves as a unit.

4–6 years

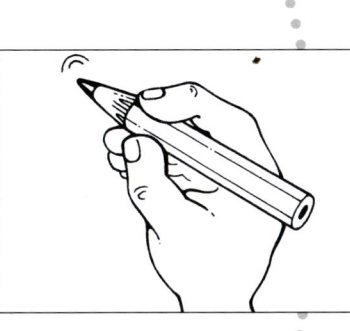

- Held with precise opposition of thumb, index and middle fingers.
- Fine, localised movements of finger joints. (Test by drawing circles.)

Cutting assessment

Name

Notes:

Date

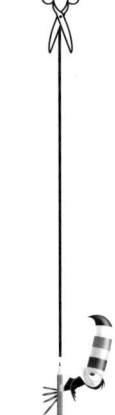

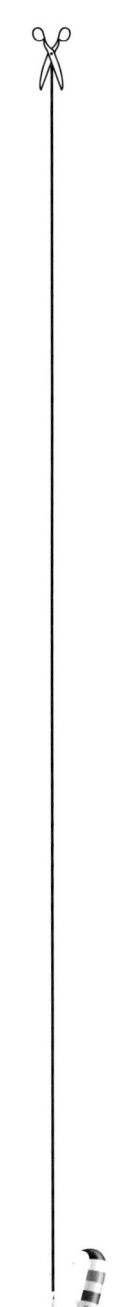

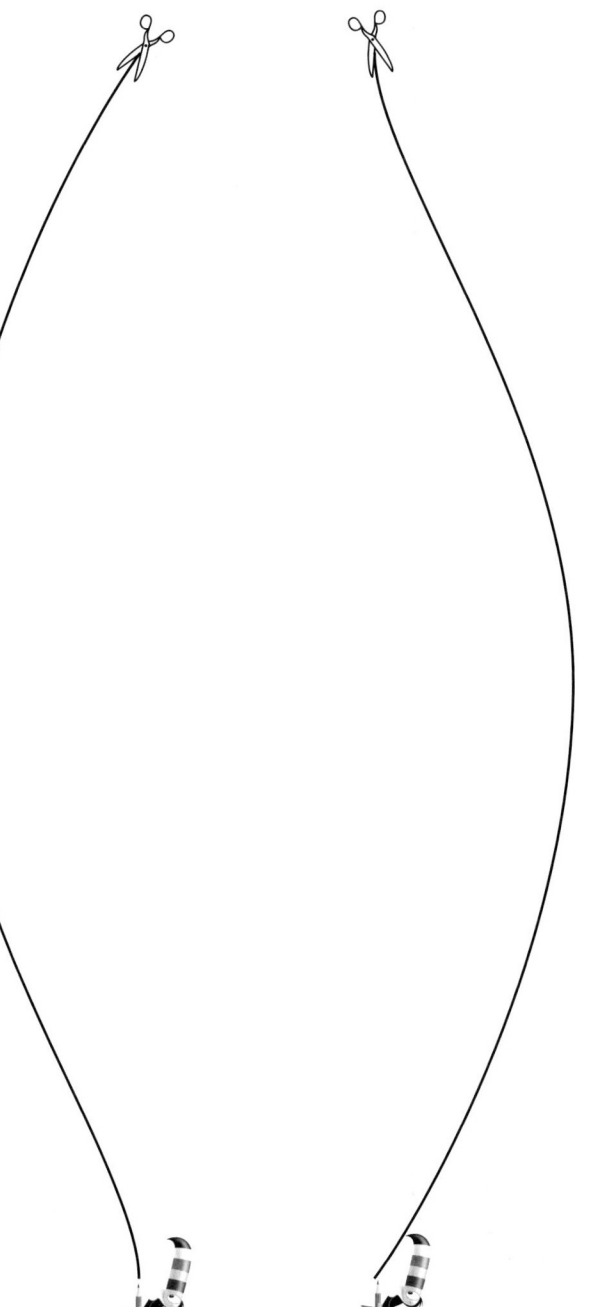

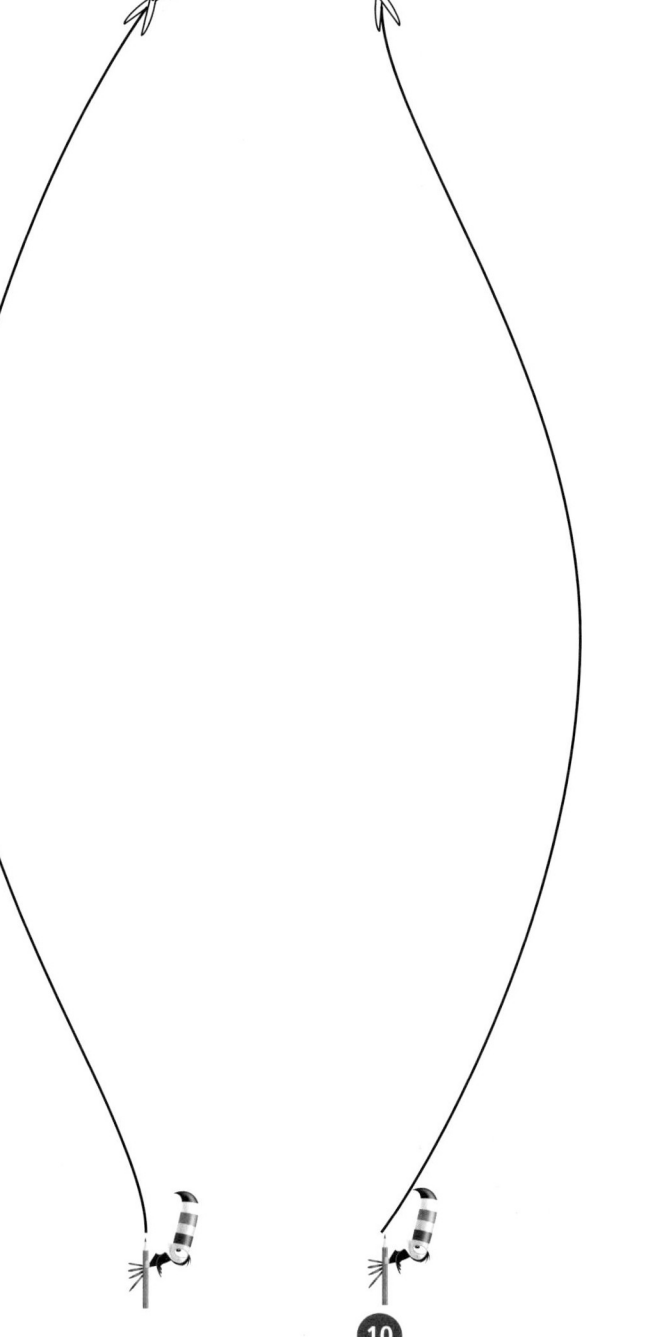

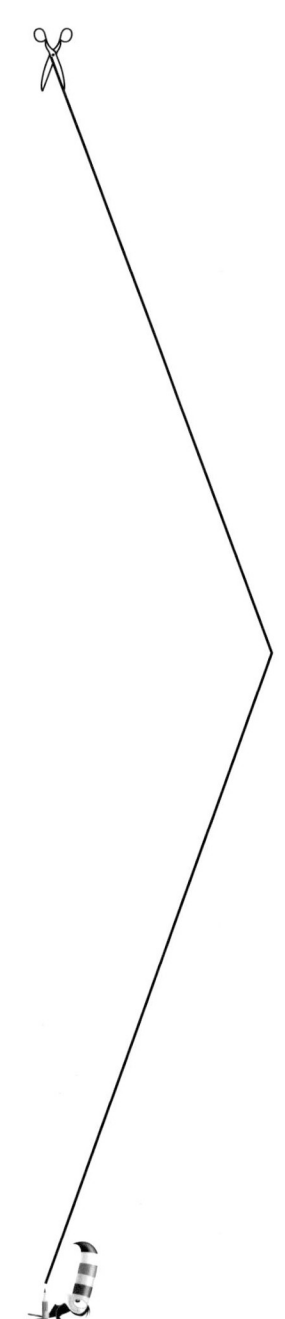

Penpals for Handwriting: Foundation 1

Handwriting pattern exercise

Name .... Date ....

Notes:

◎◎	
S	
W	
O	
ᴟ	
ᵚ	
l	

Penpals for Handwriting: Foundation 1

Children's record-keeping sheet

Name ....

Date ....

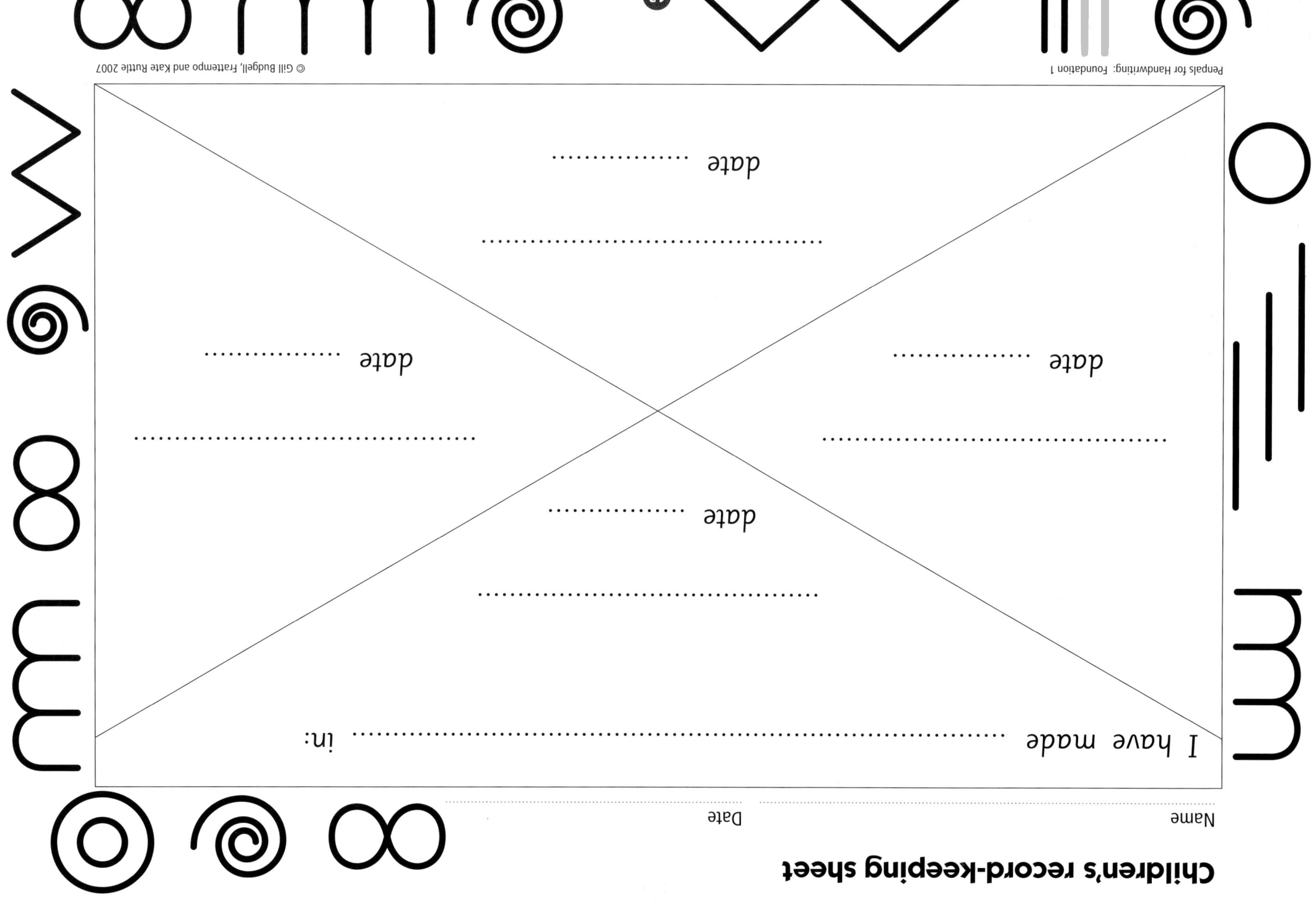

I have made .... in:

....

date ....

....

date ....

date ....

....

date ....

....

Penpals for Handwriting: Foundation 1

Glossary of key terms

Throughout *Penpals* it has been assumed that correct terminology should be used as soon as possible. In the Foundation phase, there is an emphasis on becoming familiar with vocabulary to describe parts of the hands and the language of movement as well as talking about the letter patterns and the formation of letters. In all cases it is assumed that the practitioner will use the language most appropriate to the child or group of children.

Key vocabulary

The children should work towards using and understanding the following words: *top, bottom, up, down, horizontal, vertical, diagonal, clockwise, anticlockwise.*

Young children establish pencil hold through scribbles.

Terms used specifically in Foundation include:

- **Gross motor skills** The development of controlled movements of the whole body, or limbs such as the arms or legs.

- **Fine motor skills** The development of smaller controlled movements of the hand and fingers.

- **Straight lines** Patterns that feature straight lines in any direction.

- **Upward loops or garlands**
  Patterns that feature:

- **Downward loops, bridges or arcades**
  Patterns that feature:

- **Circles** Patterns that feature circles, clockwise or anticlockwise.

- **Angled movements or zig-zags**
  Patterns that feature two or more connecting horizontal, vertical or diagonal lines.

- **Eights** Patterns that feature figures of eight in vertical or horizontal planes. The horizontal plane is very tricky.

- **Spirals** Patterns that feature centre out or outside to centre and clockwise or anticlockwise directions.

- **Long ladder letters**
  l, i, t, u, j, y

- **One-armed robot letters**
  r, b, n, h, m, k, p

- **Curly caterpillar letters**
  c, a, d, o, s, g, q, e, f

- **Zig-zag monster letters**
  z, x, v, w

Penpals for Handwriting: Information sheet for parents
Foundation 1 (3–5 year olds)

Preparation for handwriting involves developing four key areas:

- **Gross motor control**: the ability to control the body.
- **Fine motor control**: the ability to fine-tune the movements of the arm, hand and fingers.
- **Visual control**: the ability to co-ordinate hand–eye movements.
- **Spatial control**: the awareness of oneself in space, an awareness of direction (left/right) and plane (horizontal/vertical) and how to transfer that on to paper.

Here are some things you can do at home to develop these key areas:

- Play with a ball: kick, catch, throw, bounce, etc.
- Play with hoops, frisbees and stilts (the upside-down flowerpot kind).
- Encourage play on large climbing frames in parks.
- Encourage football and dance-type activities.
- Play with large-scale building kits.
- Enjoy finger rhymes.
- Encourage your child to make things and model things (cutting, sticking, moulding, cooking, sewing, threading, etc.) using a range of materials (play dough, Plasticine, wood, etc.).
- Encourage your child to experiment with a range of tools and equipment (pens, pencils, crayons, felt tips, scissors, hole punches, tweezers, etc.).
- Share jigsaw puzzles and board games.
- Provide opportunities for painting, colouring and 'making marks' on different sizes of paper.

As part of developing confidence in these key areas the children begin to explore patterns and basic letter shapes. We experiment with the following seven basic patterns, which are excellent preparation for more formal work on letter formation.

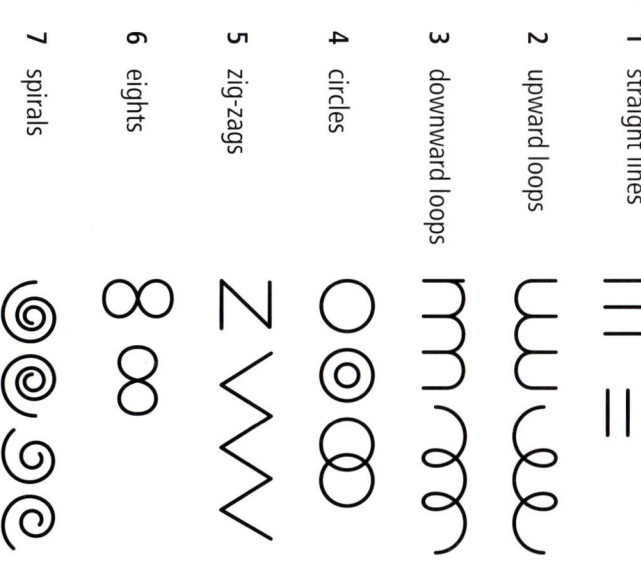

1   straight lines

2   upward loops

3   downward loops

4   circles

5   zig-zags

6   eights

7   spirals

Enjoy exploring these patterns at home in as many different ways as possible. Make patterns using paint, water, sand, flour, etc. – don't always rush to find a pencil!

Planning staff INSET

When you introduce *Penpals* into your school, it is important to ensure that all the staff in the school follow the scheme as a whole-school policy. To do this, it may be useful to hold an INSET staff meeting. The pages referenced are photocopiable to allow you to make OHTs or copies for this purpose.

'It is as though, having automated the hand, the children's minds are "liberated" to release their ideas more effectively and creatively on paper.'

Fiona Thomas, handwriting researcher and Foundation teacher

From Foundation 1 Teacher's Book

- page 9 – development of pencil hold;
- page 14 – information sheet for parents;
- page 16 – INSET OHT: preparation for handwriting in Foundation 1;
- page 17 – introduction to units: gross and fine motor skills and letter patterns.

From Foundation 2 Big Book

- inside front cover – lower case letters. (See also page 48 of this book.)

From Foundation 2 Teacher's Book

- page 4 – rationale for introducing *Penpals for Handwriting*;
- page 5 – classroom organisation;
- page 11 – information sheet for parents;
- page 60 – handwriting mats; paper position.

For information about the scheme beyond Foundation, refer to each relevant year group Teacher's Book.

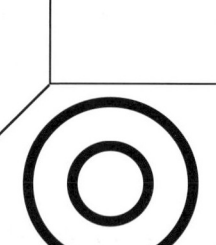

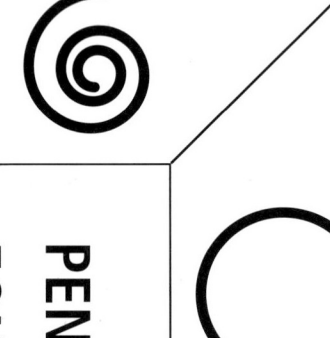

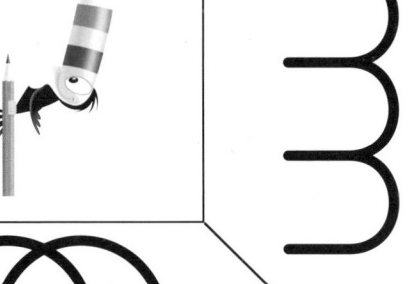

PENPALS FOR HANDWRITING
FOUNDATION 1 (3–5 YEARS)

Preparation for handwriting involves developing four key areas:

- **Gross motor control** – the ability to control the body

- **Fine motor control** – the ability to fine-tune the movements of the arm, hand and fingers

- **Visual control** – the ability to co-ordinate hand–eye movements

- **Spatial control** – the awareness of oneself in space, an awareness of direction (left/right) and plane (horizontal/vertical) and how to transfer that on to paper.

Seven basic patterns are explored in *Penpals* in preparation for basic letter formation.

Introduction to units

In order that children can eventually acquire a legible, fluent and fast handwriting style, they need to develop various skills. Visual control and spatial control are developed in all the units.

Developing gross motor skills (Units 1–3)

Gross motor control describes the development of controlled movements of the whole body, or limbs. The development of good posture and balance is crucial in relation to handwriting, as is children's awareness of the self in space. Gross motor skills are most easily developed through the physical development curriculum, which is about improving the skills of co-ordination, control, manipulation and movement.

This section offers a selection of practical ideas for developing gross motor skills and focuses on:

Unit 1   the vocabulary of movement for handwriting;
Unit 2   large movements for handwriting;
Unit 3   responding to music.

There are many more ideas and activities relating to the development of gross motor skills but these will offer a starting point.

Interactive whiteboard

See the *Penpals Foundation 1 CD-ROM* unit called 'Developing gross motor skills' for further practice of these skills.

Developing fine motor skills (Units 4–7)

Fine motor control describes the control of smaller movements of the arm, hand and fingers. Until children have gained reasonable fine motor control through a range of small-scale movements, formal handwriting and worksheets are not appropriate. A quick and useful indication of children's fine motor control is whether they can touch each finger in turn against the thumb quite quickly, either on one hand and then the other, or simultaneously.

This section offers a selection of practical ideas for developing manipulative skills and focuses on:

Unit 4   hand and finger play;
Unit 5   making and modelling;
Unit 6   links to art;
Unit 7   using one-handed tools and equipment: making marks, pencil hold, pincer movement and scissor skills.

There are many more ideas and activities relating to the development of fine motor skills but these will offer a starting point.

Interactive whiteboard

See the *Penpals Foundation 1 CD-ROM* unit called 'Developing fine motor skills' for interactive whiteboard games and activities.

Developing patterns and basic letter movements (Units 8–14)

All letters are written from patterns: the long ladder letters derive from straight lines; the one-armed robot letters derive from downward loops which form bridges; curly caterpillar letters derive from circles and the zig-zag monster letters derive from angled movements.

This section offers a selection of practical ideas for developing pattern-making skills and basic letter movement and focuses on:

Unit 8   pattern-making;
Unit 9   responding to music with pattern;
Unit 10   straight lines;
Unit 11   upward loops (garlands) and downward loops (bridges or arcades);
Unit 12   circles;
Unit 13   angled movements;
Unit 14   eights and spirals.

There are many more ideas and activities relating to the development of patterns and basic letter movements but these will offer a starting point. Some ideas templates are offered in this section for ideas and/or for children who might be ready to begin this type of pattern-making experimentation, once you have assessed that they have a reasonable level of fine motor control.

Interactive whiteboard

Each of these units is accompanied by a unit on the CD-ROM.

Penpals for Handwriting: Foundation 1

1 | Developing gross motor skills: the vocabulary of movement

Early Learning Goal links: Handwriting plus Language for communication; Movement; Music; Imagination; Responding to experiences and expressing and communicating ideas.

Ten ideas for developing the vocabulary of movement for handwriting

Focus	Contexts	Associated vocabulary
❶ Round and round	Skip round and round (individually). Hold hands and move round and round as a group. Move an object round and round – use streamers, scarves, hoops. Move arms and shoulders round and round. Move head round and round.	circles, big, small, fast, slow, this way, that way, clockwise, anticlockwise, roll
❷ Up and down	Move the whole body up and down. Climb up and down equipment. Move a streamer up and down. Move arms and shoulders up and down. Move head up and down.	high, low, above, below, stretch, curl, tall, short, reach, tiptoe, scrunch, tiny, ball
❸ Over and under	Move over and under equipment. Move whole body in waves as if going over and under objects. Make hands move under and over in waves.	up, down, high, low, through, over, under
❹ Making curves	Make curves with the whole body, standing or lying on the floor. Move both hands and then one hand in curves as if stroking a pet. Let the hands dance in waves to music.	smooth, curly, stroking, soft, gentle, over, under
❺ Making zig-zags	Make jagged movements with the body (to music). Make jagged shapes with the whole body lying on the floor. Make jagged hand movements.	up, down, sharp, jagged, points

① Round and round

⑦ Making backward, forward and sideways movements

6	Making spirals and figures of eight	Skip out from the centre of the hall in spirals and then skip in. Make both hands move in spiral movements. Make spirals with streamers and scarves. Dance in figures of eight.	out and in, in and out, round and round, snake, unfurl, uncurl, untwirl, unwind, coil, wrap up, wrap round, encircle, trap, cross over, middle
7	Making backward, forward and sideways movements	Move in different directions in a large space. Move sideways like a crab. Move both arms backwards, forwards and sideways. Make the head move sideways in different ways (looking left and right or just moving the head from side to side in a rocking motion).	in front, behind, stepping carefully, scrabble, creep, run, jump, skip, sideways, forwards, backwards
8	Standing up and lying down	Stretch body as tall as possible. Lie on floor and make body as long as possible. Crouch down to make body as short as possible. Curl up on side to make body as small as possible.	stretch, curl, tight, long, longer, tall, taller, small, smaller, short, shorter
9	Balancing and posture	Experiment with balancing on large equipment – low beams and benches. Walk along different line markings to keep balance. Walk with a bean bag on the head. Practise walking very tall as if someone is pulling up your head with a piece of string – then they let go and you collapse! Scrunch up shoulders and then relax them. Touch the chin on the chest and then lift the chin up.	tall, stretch, up, straight, pull up, look up, carefully, concentrate, use hands and arms, straight back, shoulders down, comfort, relax
10	Sky writing	Develop sky writing and encourage the use of both hands. Practise in the air, on palms and on backs. Experiment with different types of movement as outlined above (e.g. zig-zag patterns, curvy patterns).	big, sweeping, imagine, stretch, reach, draw, outline, practise

On the Penpals CD-ROM: Developing gross motor skills (Units 1, 2, 3)

Warm up
- Responding to music with appropriate body actions: Jumping jacks

Talk about
- Draw children's attention to shapes and patterns in their environment. At the same time develop the vocabulary for describing them.
- Investigate patterns, exploring: Round and round, Up and down, Over and under, Making curves, making eights and spirals, Bounce.

Try
- Guess what's hidden!
- Hit it, quick!
- Behind the blind

Penpals pad
- Let your children explore pattern-making by drawing big shapes and swooshes across the screen.

Gallery
- Add your own images of patterns your children have made – either as scans or digital photographs. You can even add images from the internet of patterns that you want to talk to the children about.

Early Learning Goal links: Handwriting plus Language for communication; Movement; Sense of space; Using equipment.

Ten ideas for developing large movements for handwriting

③ Stilts

Equipment	Benefit
❶ Balls	Holding sponge balls and squeezing strengthens finger movement and lower arm muscles. Any movement with small balls will assist with hand–eye co-ordination and the development of spatial awareness. Throwing small balls involves sweeping underarm and overarm movements. Catching small balls involves a clenching of the fingers and hands. Bouncing small balls involves using the palm of the hand in an up/down movement.
❷ Medium-sized or large hoops	This is a useful assessment tool. Left to their own devices, a group of Foundation-aged children invited to play with hoops will probably resort to three modes of behaviour. Let the children play freely with hoops and observe their play. Some behaviours may indicate 'readiness' for handwriting: 1 Propelling the hoop a distance, which involves a forward and then backward movement of the arm plus a release in order to push the hoop across the floor. Children who have this level of control are likely to be ready for learning the skills of handwriting on paper. 2 Spinning the hoop between the fingers in order to make it twirl round and round. This movement demands a high degree of finger manipulation but little force. These children are probably on the cusp of being ready for learning the skills of handwriting on paper. 3 Throwing the hoop around madly in any fashion! These children are unlikely to be ready to learn the skills of handwriting on paper and need further gross motor skill development.
❸ Stilts	The use of small plastic buckets with rope attached to either side creates a simple version of stilts. These are invaluable for the development of balance. Pulling on the rope to lift the stilt in order to move is demanding on arm muscles and is very good for building stamina.

❹	Frisbees (solid sponge or Polo sponge)	The movement of launching the frisbee from the hand in order to propel it some distance demands a pincer grip and involves a sweeping upper arm movement. The gesture of launching the frisbee through the air is supportive of the movement involved in pushing a pen or pencil across a piece of paper. This movement also aids muscle tone in the arm in preparation for handwriting and supports the development of spatial awareness.
❺	Streamers	Silk scarves or streamers on sticks can be used for more advanced movement than is possible with hoops. The manipulation of the streamer in patterns (up, down, round and round, spirals, slow, fast, on the spot, in free flight) involves the use of the wrist and is a very effective way to prepare the appropriate movements of the wrist for handwriting. Holding a scarf only is less sophisticated than holding a streamer on a stick.

④ Frisbees

The following activities are more generally helpful for developing good physical movement but will aid the necessary skills for handwriting.

❻	Climbing frames	Gripping with the arms will strengthen arm muscles and support the development of spatial awareness. Children with poor gross motor control may need to be encouraged to try and move higher than knee height. Good for practising balance and flexibility.
❼	Dance	Will support the development of rhythmic and controlled body movement depending on balance, posture, agility, co-ordination, etc. Supports spatial awareness. May help to identify dominant foot and handedness. Will support an awareness of pattern and sequence and develop listening skills.
❽	Football	Will support hand–eye co-ordination, body awareness, muscle strength, etc. Kicking may help to identify dominant foot and handedness.
❾	Cycling	Will support spatial awareness, muscle tone, hand–eye co-ordination, sense of direction and balance.
❿	Large-scale construction kits	Will support spatial awareness, muscle strength and an awareness of shape.

⑤ Streamers

'Handwriting is PE on paper'

Fiona Thomas, handwriting researcher and Foundation teacher

3 | Developing gross motor skills: responding to music

Early Learning Goal links: Handwriting plus Language for communication; Linking sounds and letters; Shape, space and measures; Movement; Sense of space; Music; Imagination; Responding to experiences and expressing and communicating ideas.

♩ ♪ ♩ ♪ *Ten musical tracks for exploring gross motor movements*

Using the CD tracks

The chart below shows how selected tracks on the CD have been assembled to provide you with a complete range of handwriting-related warm ups. Many of these movements feature in Foundation 2 as suggestions for preparing the children for the whole-class session. See page 5 for a full list of CD tracks.

Each track may be used in a number of ways:

- In the classroom as a warm up for any session where you are exploring a particular pattern. Some of the ideas, such as *Circle Time!*, may well require more space than you have available in the classroom but generally the children should be able to respond within a reasonable space.
- In the hall or playground as a warm up to a music and movement lesson.

You may choose to use the 3–4 minute warm up on its own or you may choose to use it alongside another track in order to contrast the patterns and movements. On a wet Friday afternoon you may choose to play all the tracks and let the children respond in their own way! It is important for them to be able to hear the differences in the music and to respond accordingly.

The tracks invite specific movements relating to the gross motor movements that we know will support the children's general physical development as well as ensuring readiness for finer motor movements and then handwriting.

Target movement	Relates to unit . . .	Music ♩ ♪ ♩ ♪
Whole-body rhymes	1, 2	❶ *If You're Happy and You Know it* (Track 1)
Making straight lines	1, 2, 10	❷ *Marching* (Track 2) ❸ *Growing and Shrinking* (Track 3)
Bouncing	1, 2, 11	❹ *Bounces, Springs, Jumps and Skips!* (Track 4)
Exploring ring games and circles	1, 2, 12	❺ *Circle Time!* (Track 5) (Ring a Ring a Roses) (**NB:** You may need to point out the difference between clockwise and anticlockwise.) ❻ *This Way and That* (Track 6) (Children dance round an object and pretend it's a maypole. You could attach gymnastic ribbons or crepe paper strips to the object for added effect.)

Making round, flowing movements	1, 2, 12, 14	❼ *Twist and Curl* (You could use hoops here.) (Track 7)
Exploring angled movements	1, 2, 13	❽ *Karate* (Track 8)
Making spirals and figures of eight	1, 2, 14	❾ *Swing Your Partner* (Track 9)
		❿ *Twist and Spiral* (Track 10) (If you have access to a spiralling wind mobile, this demonstrates the movement wonderfully.)

Track ⑧

Track ⑩

Using percussion instruments

Children can use their whole bodies or adapt the movement for arms and fingers only.

Target movement	Suggested instrument
Fast and slow	Use a tambourine. Rattle it or drum quickly for children to run on the spot; tap it slowly for slower movement.
Heavy and light	Use a rainstick and a drum. Let the children move on tiptoes for the light sound of the rainstick and plod heavily to the sound of the drum.
Up and down	Use a triangle. Rattle the beater inside the triangle while children jump up and run anticlockwise. When you hit the triangle they sit down quickly. Repeat going clockwise.
High and low	Use two chime bars. As you hit the higher one, children stretch up high; when you play the lower one, they crouch down low.
Grow and shrink	Use a glockenspiel or xylophone. Children listen and grow tall as you move towards the longer, lower notes and shrink as you move up the scale.
Long and short	Use a guiro. Children make long snakes on the floor, wiggling as you make long sounds. When you tap, using short sounds, they make shorter snakes.
Skip and jump	Use a drum. Tap out rhythms for skipping or jumping.

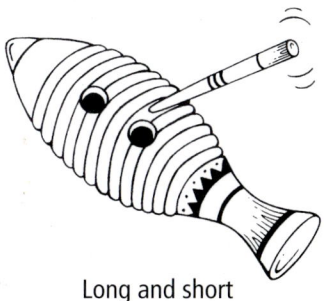

Long and short

Developing fine motor skills: hand and finger play

Early Learning Goal links: Handwriting plus Language for communication; Linking sounds and letters; Movement; Music; Responding to experiences and expressing and communicating ideas.

Ten ideas for hand and finger play

Action rhymes and finger rhymes are an obvious way to help children explore the movement (stretch, curl, bend, clench, unfurl, point, etc.) and the language of hands (palms, fingers, thumbs, wrists, index, knuckles, etc.). Exercising fingers in preparation for handwriting is important as small children may find it physically tiring to hold pens and pencils – they often grip too tightly. The rhymes below are suggested for practising different hand and finger movements, but there are many, many more. Consider building a few of these into a routine so that the children adopt the habit of warming up the hands and fingers in preparation for handwriting. You may just want to do them because they're fun! These rhymes are sung on the Foundation 1 CD and the words of the rhymes are printed on page 46. See page 5 for a full list of CD tracks.

Finger puppets will encourage participation. Use socks, gloves, paper, fabric, etc. or just draw faces on the end of the fingers!

Focus of rhyme	Suggested rhyme(s)/action	Notes for hand actions
❶ Warming up hands and arms	Make shapes with fingers (triangle, diamond, oval, circle). Make letter shapes with fingers (e.g. *C, O*). **a** *The Wheels on the Bus* (Track 11)	Make circles (with thumb and forefingers for wheels) and diagonals (raised forefingers for wipers), waggle all fingers (fingers to thumbs opening and closing to show mouths moving for chattering people), etc.
	b *Grandmother's Glasses* (Track 12)	Hands up to eyes in circles. Hands on head. Clap hands. Interweave fingers and rest.
❷ Working on co-ordination of body actions and brain	**a** *Peter Hammers* (Track 13)	Use arms with clenched fists, one at a time, then left leg, then right leg, then nod head too.
	b *Heads, Shoulders, Knees and Toes* (Track 14)	Touch head, shoulders, knees and toes as you sing.
❸ Working on contrast: speed, rhythm	*Slowly, Slowly* (Track 15)	Walk hand slowly up your arm, then quickly run it up and down for the mouse.

② Working on co-ordination of body actions and brain

④ Working on fine control

❹	Working on fine control	**a**	*Incy Wincy Spider* (Track 16)	Make fingers walk up opposite forearm, like a spider. Raise hands and wiggle fingers for rain. Raise hands and make a wide circle for sun. Repeat first action to finish.
		b	*Here is the Church* (Track 17)	Interlace fingers, point index fingers, open thumbs, turn hands over and wiggle fingertips.
❺	Rhymes for straight lines	**a**	*Tommy Thumb* (Track 18)	Show each finger as you sing.
		b	*Five Little Peas* (Track 19)	Clasp one hand round the other, raise thumbs, straighten each pair of fingers in turn, slowly move hands apart and clap!
❻	Rhymes for round, flowing movements	**a**	*Firework* (© Tony Mitton) (Track 20)	Scribble with index finger in the air. Make hands twist and turn and flow. Put hands together and launch into the air in an outward movement to exercise shoulders.
		b	*In and Out the Dusty Bluebells* (Track 21)	Move hand in wave motion (up and down).
❼	Rhymes for circles, loops and garlands	**a**	*The Wheels on the Bus* (Track 11)	The wheels on the bus (make circles for wheels), the wipers on the bus (make index fingers move back and forth), etc.
		b	*Round and Round the Garden* (Track 22)	Circle palm, walk fingers up one arm for count of five, then tickle self.
❽	Rhymes for zig-zag movements		*Jack and Jill* (Track 23)	Zig-zag with index finger in a horizontal or vertical plane in rhythm to the rhyme.
❾	Rhymes for eights (and spirals)		*In and Out the Dusty Bluebells* (Track 21)	Move hand in figure of eight.
❿	Clapping, tapping and fists		*One Potato, Two Potato* (Track 24)	Move fists up and down to bang against each other.
			Adapt *Peter Hammers* (taps, claps, etc.) (Track 13)	

On the Penpals CD-ROM: Developing fine motor skills (Units 4, 5, 6, 7)

Warm up
- Responding to music with appropriate body actions: Exploring the hand

Talk about
- Draw children's attention to the shapes and patterns in their environment. At the same time develop the vocabulary for describing them.
- Investigate patterns, exploring: Finger patterns and shapes, Clapping, tapping and fists, Speed and rhythm, Round and flowing, Dots, Mixed patterns.

Try
- Hit it, quick!
- Join them up
- Copy the marks

Penpals pad
- Let your children explore pattern-making by drawing dots and spots.

Gallery
- Add your own images of patterns your children have made – either as scans or digital photographs. You can even add images from the internet of patterns that you want to talk to the children about.

Early Learning Goal links: Handwriting plus Language for communication; Design and making skills; Using tools and materials; Exploring media and materials; Imagination; Responding to experiences and expressing and communicating ideas.

Ten ideas for developing handwriting through making and modelling

Activities (many of these activities involve both gross and fine motor skills)	Actions	Associated handwriting language (use opportunities to talk about 'language of the hands', e.g. palm, knuckles)	Try …
Hard materials:			
❶ Using a tool-kit and pieces of wood	hammering	straight lines, up, down	• capital letters 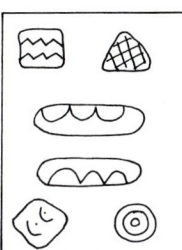
	sawing	back and forth, backwards and forwards, away, towards	• long ladders
	screwing	turn, clockwise, anticlockwise, the other way	• zig-zags
❷ Construction	building, connecting, manipulating, lifting, lining up, levelling	up, down, high, low, left, right, under	• patterns with straight lines
Pliable materials:			
❸ Cooking	kneading	down, press	• Making letter-shaped biscuits.
	rolling with rolling pin, hands or fingers	away, towards, press, pressure	• Making biscuits/cakes and decorating them with tubes of icing or different shaped decorations. Decorate the biscuit shapes with different handwriting patterns.
	whisking	round and round, clockwise, anticlockwise, the other way	
	using cutters	space, fingers, spread out	

③ Decorate biscuits with handwriting patterns

4 Play dough (soft) **5** Plasticine (hard) **6** Clay (sticky and hard but may change form if water is added)	kneading and moulding Plasticine will strengthen the muscles more effectively as it is harder and requires more force. making sausages pressing flat or rolling out flat	press, pressure, away, towards, round and round, clockwise, anticlockwise, the other way, space, fingers, spread out, carve, scratch, rub, scrape, make holes, etc.	• Making patterns and letters. • Making models (e.g. people, a park). • Making a series of laminated mats that feature letter shapes and patterns. Encourage the children to overlay the patterns with their Plasticine or dough. • Push objects and tools into it to make patterns.

④ Laminated mats featuring letter shapes and patterns

Precision, control and pincer grip: **7** Sewing **8** Weaving **9** Threading	pincer hold if using a bodkin or similar hand–eye co-ordination to control the up/down, push/pull repetition of sewing or threading dexterity if alternating strips of paper or fabric for weaving	up, down, back again hold under, over, round and round	• Using plastic coffee stirrers from fast food chains for threading. • Making pom-poms by winding wool round and round two Polo-shaped pieces of card. When quite fat with wool, snip all the way round the edge. Tie tightly in between the two pieces of card before removing them. • Children sew over their names with a bodkin needle and wool on a clean polystyrene tray. • Weaving with long strips of paper and then sticking the weaving behind cut-outs of pattern or letter shapes on black sugar paper. • Making short and long pasta necklaces: use straight, spiral or wheel pasta. • Threading buttons on to strings. • Making sequences or matching patterns to those given on laminated cards.

Making pom-poms

⑧ Weaving

10 Collage	pincer movement for picking up and sorting; pushing down, gluing	big, small, up, down, high, low, left, right, under	• Making different textures.

Early Learning Goal links: Handwriting plus Language for communication; Language for thinking; Design and making skills; Using tools and materials; Exploring media and materials; Imagination; Responding to experiences and expressing and communicating ideas.

Ten ideas for developing handwriting through links to art

Pattern		Link to an artist and a representative painting
Straight lines Use bold colours to paint the solid squares.	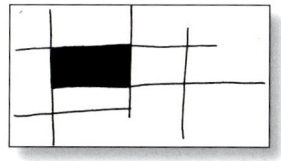	❶ Piet Mondrian (1872–1944) Dutch *Composition in Red, Yellow and Blue* (1921)
Use pencils or charcoal to experiment with different lines.		❷ William Hogarth (1697–1764) English *The Enraged Musician* (1741) Scenes of everyday life using lines (hatching) or criss-cross lines (cross-hatching).
Short, rough lines Use paint and draw short, rough lines.		❸ André Derain (1880–1954) French *Charing Cross Bridge* (1906)
Round, flowing movements Use thick paint and fingers.		❹ Vincent van Gogh (1853–1890) Dutch *Starry Night* (1889)
Dots Use blobs of colour (thick paint) to make flowers on a green background.	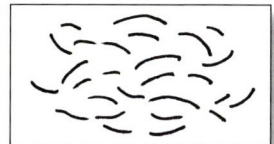	❺ Claude Monet (1840–1926) French *The Water-lily Pond* (1899)

Wassily Kandinsky (1866–1944) Russian
Swinging (1925)

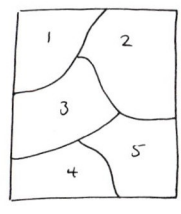

Technique 1: Looking at the whole painting

Kandinsky uses line, shape, colour and symbols to express his feelings and ideas.
Talk about the painting:
What colours can you see?
What shapes can you see?
Who can find a big (circle) and a small (circle)?
Who can point to a straight line/a curved line/wavy lines?
Show me two shapes that touch or overlap.
Can you see anything that looks as though it's swinging?

Technique 2: Revealing the picture section by section

Cut a piece of sugar paper into about five pieces and Blu-Tack these on top of the painting like jigsaw pieces. Slowly reveal each section of the painting and discuss each one. This technique focuses on interpretation and tends to support modelling of the shapes and patterns revealed.
Two days later, see if the children can repeat the process. You will be amazed at how much they have remembered about the painting.

Use cotton buds with paint to fill in the outline of a shape in dots.

6 Georges Seurat (1859–1891)
French
Sunday Afternoon on the Isle of the Grande Jatte (1884)

Circles, loops and garlands

Use paints, chalks or crayons to make circles, loops and garlands. Use different colours to make rainbow arches.

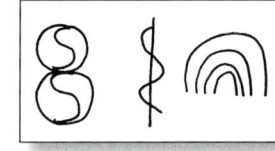

7 Robert Delaunay (1885–1941)
French
Rhythm without End (1933) (circles),
Saint-Severin No. 5 The Rainbow (1909) (arches)

Overlap circles on large pieces of paper.

8 Wassily Kandinsky (1866–1944)
Russian
Several Circles (1926)

Eights and spirals

Use green, red, purple, yellow, orange and blue.

9 Henri Matisse (1869–1954)
French
The Snail (1953)

Fill an outline with eights and spirals using gold paint.

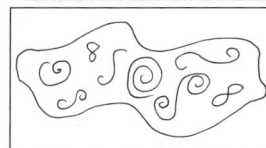

10 Gustav Klimt (1862–1918)
Austrian
Mother and Child, The Kiss (1907)

Note that Joan Miró (1893–1983), the Spanish Surrealist painter, is also excellent for exploring a combination of these patterns.

Generic activities

1 Encourage the children to draw or paint pictures that use the same shapes and patterns as Kandinsky, or the artist you have chosen.

2 Prepare lots of collage pieces in different colours, sizes and shapes for the children to use to make a collage in the style of Kandinsky, or the artist you have chosen.

3 Encourage the children to play with bricks of different colours, shapes and sizes to make a large-scale picture on the floor.

4 Children do single shape pictures – they choose the shape or pattern they like best from the painting and use it in their own picture (any medium).

5 Make shapes and fix to a straw using cotton or string so that the children can swing them through the air.

6 Give the children a geometric shape and ask them to fill it with all the shapes and patterns they can see in the painting.

7 Make a collaborative class pattern where each child completes a section.

7 | Developing fine motor skills: using one-handed tools and equipment

Early Learning Goal links: Handwriting plus Language for communication; Writing; Using equipment; Using tools and materials; Exploring media and materials; Music; Responding to experiences and expressing and communicating ideas.

Ten ideas for using one-handed tools and equipment for developing handwriting

Equipment	Movement benefit	Activities
❶ Dustpan and brush	The hand grasps the handle of the brush whilst there is a sweeping arm movement towards (or away from) the body. This will support the notion of clockwise or anticlockwise movements.	Spill sand out on to a flat surface outside. Encourage the children to sweep it into patterns. They may sweep it away or towards them. They may choose to make garlands or loops. All will be good for developing strength in the arm. They can also practise this movement whilst tidying up!
❷ Jugs and teapots	The hand grasps the handle of the jug whilst there is a lifting arm movement in a vertical direction. This supports the pattern of straight lines and hand–eye co-ordination.	Put jugs in the water tray and encourage the filling of vessels from great arm heights! The arm goes up and the water falls down. Try different types of jugs with different handles and spouts. Ask children to experiment with pouring other things such as flour, sand and glue. What patterns are made when these are poured?
❸ Hole punch or stamper	The hand or hands push down with the force of the body. Handwriting does not generally require a downward force but many letters are formed with a downward movement.	Under supervision, allow children to experiment with punching holes in paper, punching holes over lines to make a pattern or making small books.
❹ Pegs	The thumb and index finger work together in a pincer movement that supports the traditional pencil hold. The pincer movement strengthens the hand muscles that will assist pencil hold and control for writing.	Provide strips of card and lots of different types of pegs. Encourage the children to make constructions using the pegs to fix the pieces of card together. Alternatively, encourage the children to make patterns by clipping the pegs along the edge of the card. Allow the children to make collections on washing lines in the classroom (e.g. doll's clothes, socks, number lines, paintings).
❺ Tweezers	Like pegs, tweezers support the development of the pincer grip but also involve arm movement. The objects being moved are small, so this activity also supports the development of hand–eye co-ordination.	Put sequins, buttons or paper clips in a bowl to be sorted into types (by colour, size, etc.). Provide the children with an outline of a shape. They run glue around the outside of the shape and then use tweezers to pick up sequins or similar to place on the glued edge to make an outline picture.

① Dustpan and brush

② Jugs and teapots

④ Pegs

30

❻ Peg boards	Peg boards also provide excellent pincer movement practice just by using the thumb and finger.	Set out various types of peg board. Plastic boards shaped into a recognisable object on to which you place tiny coloured plastic tubes (Hama beads) are excellent for this level of fine motor control. Also use board games that involve the picking up and moving of counters.
❼ Scissors (scissors with springs/two holes enable adults to support developing skills)	Scissor control needs lots of practice and demands control of hand muscles to open and close them. Left-handers must have left-handed scissors.	Ask children to practise the opening and closing action of the thumb and fingers without scissors to feel the correct movement. Once the correct movement is established, work on holding the scissors in the correct way – talk about where the thumb goes, where the fingers go and which way up to hold the scissors. With care, look at the blades (if you have scissors with blades). Then look at the positioning of the hand and scissors in relation to the paper. Talk about how you can turn the paper round to help you. Provide simple patterns for children to cut along.
❽ Mouse control (**NB:** Small mice are available from some firms.)	Using a mouse develops hand muscles and hand–eye co-ordination. It also encourages an awareness of direction.	All Foundation classrooms should have access to computers. There are many Early Years programmes for developing mouse control and basic concepts of left, right and orientation.
❾ Magnet pathways	Holding the magnet and pressing up. Hand is invisible to the eye, so must follow the movement of the magnetic toy.	Construct a simple pathway on thick cardboard. Children should follow the pathway using a magnetic toy on top and a magnet below (e.g. a car on a road, a snail following a trail).
❿ Making marks: writing tools and pencil hold	Experimenting with different types of writing implements will help children to find a hold that is comfortable and efficient.	Ask children to make patterns on bars of soap by scratching, filing, rubbing, scraping, etc. As above but try using blocks of plaster. Include different types and thicknesses of paint brushes, glue spatulas, chalk, felt pens, crayons, crayon pencils and pencils as well as less obvious mark-making tools such as cotton buds (for dotting), rulers, lollipop sticks, combs (for scraping) and bricks (for printing). Allow children to paint outside walls with water. Encourage imaginative play in role play areas by always providing for mark-making and writing. Many situations in life involve these skills! Be aware that the traditional pencil hold is as shown here and, while there is no absolute right and wrong, it is generally acknowledged that a traditional pencil hold enables children to develop a controlled and fluent handwriting style over time. Be aware of left-handers and help them to adopt a pencil hold that is both comfortable and efficient.

⑥ Peg boards

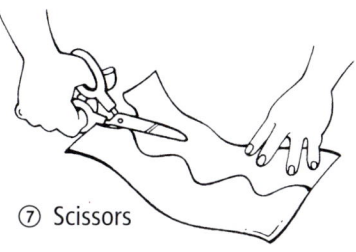

⑦ Scissors

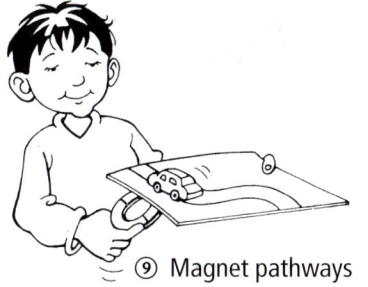

⑨ Magnet pathways

⑩ Making marks

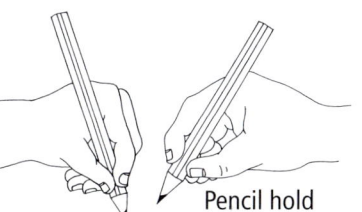

Pencil hold

Developing patterns and basic letter movements: pattern-making

Early Learning Goal links: Handwriting plus Language for communication; Language for thinking; Shape, space and measures; Exploration and investigation.

Ten ideas for developing pattern

❶ Make cross-curricular links by talking about patterns in PE, music, art, number work and stories. Look for patterns in the environment.

❷ Allow the children to experiment with pattern at gross and fine motor levels by using some of the ideas set out in the previous units of this book. Children must be ready to pick up a pencil or pen in order to work at fine motor skill level.

❸ Sky writing patterns in the air or writing patterns on each other's backs keeps the gross motor skill awareness at the forefront of the experience so that confidence is gained.

❹ Writing the patterns in paint or sand, making them in play dough and pretend writing on the children's palms will all help to keep the fine motor skill awareness at the forefront of the experience so that confidence is gained.

❺ Use the language of handwriting with the children so that they develop the oral skills to talk about pattern and feel confident enough to experiment.

❻ Go on a pattern-finding walkabout and encourage the children to record the patterns they find, for example fences, paving stones, flowers, zebra crossings.

❼ Draw out a large-scale 3 x 3 grid and encourage the children to fill each square with a different kind of pattern using chalks. Alternatively, use the same idea to produce a large-scale class painting.

❽ Draw ten one-metre-long lines in the playground and encourage the children to put a pattern on/under/across each one using chalks.

❾ Make pattern boards for each pattern family (straight lines, upward and downward loops, circles and angled movements) from card and laminate them. Using the ideas template (page 33), encourage the children to make printed patterns in the owl using items of different shapes and sizes (e.g. cotton buds, fingers, cotton reels, matchbox ends, etc.).

❿ Talk about straight lines, upward loops (garlands) and downward loops (bridges or arcades), circles, angled movements, spirals, eights, short, long, big and small, etc.

⑦

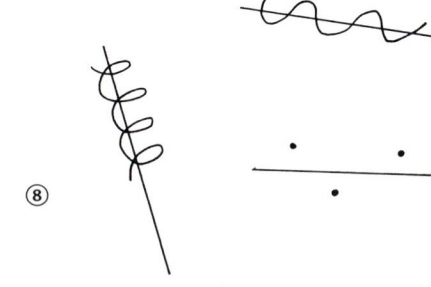

⑧

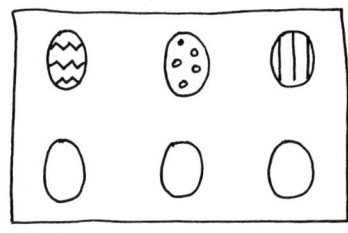

⑨

Make patterns in the owl.

 On the Penpals CD-ROM: Pattern-making

Warm up
- Hand patterns

Talk about
- Draw children's attention to the shapes and patterns in their environment whilst developing the vocabulary for describing them.
- Children can find patterns: Patterns inside, Patterns outside, Looking up, Looking down, Body patterns, Animal patterns.

Try
- Follow the dot to make a pattern
- Jigsaw
- Trace over the patterns

Penpals pad
- Let your children explore pattern making. Encourage them to be as inventive as they can and create lots of different patterns.

Gallery
- Add your own images of patterns your children have made – either as scans or digital photographs. You can even add images from the internet of patterns that you want to talk to the children about.

Early Learning Goal links: Handwriting plus Language for communication; Shape, space and measures; Movement; Sense of space; Music; Imagination; Responding to experiences and expressing and communicating ideas.

Ten musical tracks for exploring patterns and basic letter movements

Target pattern	Music ♩♪♩
Making straight lines (Units 1, 2, 10)	❶ *Shooting Stars* (Track 25) Short, staccato sounds for short lines – left to right or up/down, diagonal. Long, stretched sound for long lines – left to right or up/down, diagonal. Alternating the two – shooting stars.
Exploring upward loops (garlands) and downward loops (bridges or arcades) (Units 1, 2, 11, 12)	❷ *The Seaside* (Track 26) Children make the waves on the sea – sea music. Children put the seagulls in the sky – bird sounds.
Exploring circles (Units 1, 2, 12)	❸ *Space* (Track 27) Children make the sun and moon – space music. ❹ *Ripples* (Track 28) Ripples on water.
Making round, flowing movements (Units 1, 2, 12, 14)	❺ *Kite Flying* (Track 29) Meandering music.

You need:

- a CD player
- a big piece of paper – A3 or larger (This can be sugar paper or a piece cut from a roll of paper.)
- space for the children to work freely without being restricted by bumping into others, or space to work collaboratively whilst sitting or standing at tables or kneeling on the floor (You may choose to do these activities with smaller groups in a separate area or room.)
- Blu-Tack for securing the edges of paper during pattern-making
- a range of chalks, coloured pens, pencils and brushes, depending on your chosen medium.

Using the CD tracks

The chart on the left shows how selected tracks on the CD have been assembled to provide you with a complete range of handwriting-related activities. The activities assume a certain level of readiness for exploring fine motor control skills but the stress is on allowing children to listen and respond imaginatively. Feeling the movement is an important step towards confidence and fluidity in mark-making. Closing their eyes may help the children to concentrate on the movement. See the inside front cover for a full list of CD tracks.

Each track may be used in a number of ways:

- in the classroom as a whole-class experience
- in the classroom or elsewhere as a group activity.

You may choose to use a couple of tracks consecutively in order to contrast the patterns and movements that they evoke. You may choose to play all the tracks and let the children respond in their own way! It is important for them to be able to hear the differences in the music and to respond accordingly.

Exploring angled movements (Units 1, 2, 13)	❻	*Dinosaur Land* (Track 30) Children draw spikes on the dinosaur's back, zig-zag teeth, zig-zag mountains.
Making figures of eight (Units 1, 2, 14)	❼	*Train Track* (Track 31) Music for horizontal figure of eight.
Making spirals (Units 1, 2, 14)	❽	*Spirals* (Track 32) Music starts with a quiet sound and children make the spiral grow as the music grows. Music starts with a loud sound and children make the spiral shrink as the music shrinks.
Combinations (all units)	❾	*Firework Night* (Track 33)
	❿	*Animal Moves* (Track 34)

Moving

The tracks invite specific movements relating to the fine motor movements and patterns that we know will support the children's general physical development as well as ensuring readiness for finer motor movements and then handwriting. The music and patterns suggest a context or story which is offered as support for the mark-making and not as a constraint. The activity is about movements and not a finished picture so, in this way, every response is acceptable. Occasionally, you may need to hold a child's hands to help them to feel the pattern. This is of particular importance for children with immature co-ordination.

Stop the music from time to time for discussion or clarification and don't be afraid to repeat sections if the children are enjoying the movement or need further practice. Finding the flow and the rhythm will take several sessions.

Encourage the children to use both hands simultaneously or either hand in different situations (whichever is comfortable).

Posture and desk height do not matter at this stage since it is the focus on the movement that is paramount.

 On the Penpals CD-ROM: Responding to music

Warm up
- Responding to music with appropriate body actions: Move it!

Talk about
- Draw children's attention to the aural shapes and patterns in music and in their environment. At the same time develop visual patterns in response and the vocabulary for describing them.
- Investigate patterns: Straight lines, Loops, Circles, Round and flowing, Angled and spiky lines, Twist-and-turn spirals.

Try
- Responding to music
- Listen to the music and guess what's hidden
- Musical toucans

Penpals pad
- Let your children explore pattern-making. Can they draw patterns for their favourite songs?

Gallery
- Add your own images of patterns your children have made – either as scans or digital photographs. You can even add images from the internet of patterns that you want to talk to the children about.

Early Learning Goal links: Handwriting plus Language for communication; Language for thinking; Writing; Shape, space and measures; Exploration and investigation; Movement; Using tools and materials; Exploring media and materials.

Ten ideas for investigating straight line patterns

❶ Make cross-curricular links by talking about straight lines in PE, music, art and number work. Look for straight lines in the environment.

❷ In PE, encourage children to walk tall, stretch out in straight lines, walk in straight lines.
Sky writing straight lines in the air or writing lines on each other's backs keeps the gross motor skill awareness at the forefront of the experience so that confidence is gained.

❸ Use the language of handwriting with the children so that they develop the oral skills to talk about pattern and feel confident enough to experiment. Talk about short lines, long lines, top to bottom (vertical) lines, and left to right (horizontal) lines and even diagonal and fanned lines.

❹ Children paint, drag or print straight line patterns using corrugated cardboard – or try painting on corrugated cardboard to give a backdrop of straight lines.

❺ Children paint straight line tracks using cars and trucks whose wheels have been dipped in paint. They make the lines criss-cross – but don't allow any curves!

❻ Children paint lines – from top to bottom or from left to right. The lines can cross each other. On a dry day, take a selection of brushes outside and let the children paint walls with water. They reach up high to make high straight lines, but encourage them to make horizontal lines too.

❼ Working with paints of all colours, encourage the children to paint old pieces of string. They'll find it quite tricky to paint these as they are small and rounded. Once dry, the pieces of string can be mounted on to a backdrop (wood would be ideal) in patterns of straight lines.
NB: the pieces of painted string can be re-used for different patterns at a later date if they are not fixed.

❽ Encourage the children to experiment with long and short straight lines using the ideas template (page 37). They should use a pencil or thin felt tip and should always start from the top or the left.

❾ The drawings on the right provide further ideas for exploring straight line patterns in any medium.

❿ Talk about the long ladder letters that are written from a straight line beginning: l, i, t, u, j, y. Notice that they all begin with a straight line but then have other features (curves, curls, descenders, etc.). *Penpals: Foundation 2* deals with the teaching of these letters.

⑨ Explore the straight line patterns.

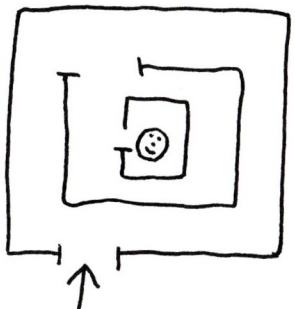

Follow the trail.

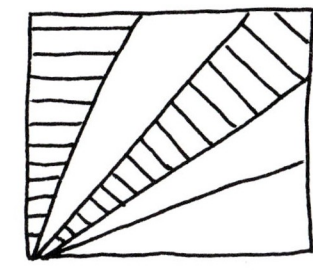

Finish the pattern.

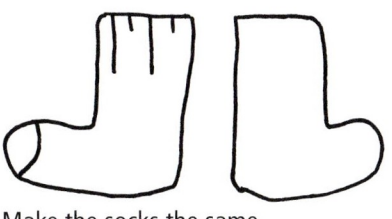

Make the socks the same.

Trace the patterns.

Make patterns on the fish.

On the Penpals CD-ROM:
Investigating straight line patterns

Warm up
- Gross and fine motor skills: Zips

Talk about
- Draw your children's attention to the straight lines in their environment whilst developing the vocabulary for describing them.
- Children can find patterns: Patterns inside and out, Looking up and down, Body patterns, Animal patterns.
- Talk about the long ladder letters: l, i, t, u, y, j.

Try
- Finish the pattern
- Copy the marks
- Musical toucans

Penpals pad
- Encourage children to create their own patterns and drawings using straight lines.

Gallery
- Add your own images of patterns your children have made – either as scans or digital photographs. You can even add images from the internet of patterns that you want to talk to the children about.

Early Learning Goal links: Handwriting plus Language for communication; Language for thinking; Writing; Shape, space and measures; Exploration and investigation; Movement; Using tools and materials; Exploring media and materials.

Ten ideas for investigating loops

❶ Make cross-curricular links by talking about loops in PE, music, art and number work. Look for loops in the environment – on top of railings, on bridges, in windows, etc.

❷ In PE, encourage children to mirror the bridge pattern by making a bridge or arch. Can they 'bunny hop' to reinforce the idea of the repetitive loop?
Sky writing loops in the air or writing loops on each other's backs keeps the gross motor skill awareness at the forefront of the experience so that confidence is gained.

❸ Use the language of handwriting with the children so that they develop the oral skills to talk about pattern and feel confident enough to experiment. Talk about upward loops (garlands) and downward loops (bridges or arcades) and going over. Always encourage the children to start the patterning at the top (even on a downward loop).

❹ Working with thick white paste, children use their fingers to make loop patterns on the table. They might also try using forks or small combs. Children could also use large brushes and water to paint loops on a paved area outside.

❺ Children paint looping tracks using cars and trucks whose wheels have been dipped in paint. They make the cars reverse for the 'bounce back up' movement of the upward loop.

❻ Cut out upward and downward loop patterns from sandpaper. Encourage the children to feel the patterns – taking care as the sandpaper will scratch. Then encourage them to paint a loop pattern within the sandpaper – they'll notice that it's quite tricky to paint on this rough surface. It will give an interesting effect.

❼ Children make paper chains and loop them around the classroom to show the upward loop (garland). It will be harder to demonstrate the downward loop but if enough children hold on at various points then it should be possible!
Alternatively, children make garland patterns in chalk on the playground.

❽ Encourage the children to experiment with big and small loops using the ideas template (page 39). They should use a pencil or thin felt tip and should always start at the top.

❾ The drawings on the right provide further ideas for exploring looped patterns in any medium.

❿ Talk about the one-armed robot letters that are written from a downward loop (bridge or arcade) beginning: r, b, n, h, m, k, p. Notice that these letters all begin with a downward movement that bounces back up but they have other features too (curves, flicks, descenders, ascenders, etc). Notice that although u begins with a straight line it is actually like an upward loop. *Penpals: Foundation 2* deals with the teaching of all these letters.

⑨ Complete the patterns.

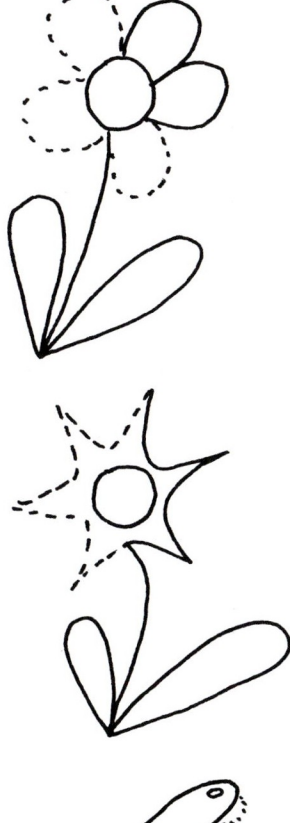

Trace the patterns.

Make patterns on the balloons.

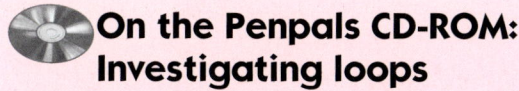 **On the Penpals CD-ROM: Investigating loops**

Warm up
- Gross and fine motor skills: Storm at sea

Talk about
- Draw children's attention to the loops in their environment whilst developing the vocabulary for describing them.
- Children can find patterns: Patterns inside and out, Looking up and down, Body patterns, Animal patterns.
- Talk about the one-armed robot letters: r, n, m, p, h, k, b.

Try
- Follow the dot to make a pattern
- Join the dots
- Guess what's hidden!

Penpals pad
- Let your children explore pattern-making. Get them to experiment with drawing loops in different colours or with different pens.

Gallery
- Add your own images of patterns your children have made – either as scans or digital photographs. You can even add images from the internet of patterns that you want to talk to the children about.

Early Learning Goal links: Handwriting plus Language for communication; Language for thinking; Writing; Shape, space and measures; Exploration and investigation; Movement; Using tools and materials; Exploring media and materials.

Ten ideas for investigating circles

❶ Make cross-curricular links by talking about circles in PE, music, art and number work. Look for circles in the environment – wheels, windows, letter O on signs, etc.

❷ In PE, encourage children to make circles and dance both anticlockwise and clockwise. Encourage children to run round hoops in both directions too. Make small circles and big circles. Sky writing circles in the air or writing circles on each other's backs keeps the gross motor skill awareness at the forefront of the experience so that confidence is gained.

❸ Use the language of handwriting with the children so that they develop the oral skills to talk about pattern and feel confident enough to experiment. Talk about circles, going round in different directions (clockwise and anticlockwise), completing the circle, etc. Always encourage the patterning to start in the position of about one o'clock.

❹ Using a foam tube (the type used to insulate central heating pipes), children dip the end into paint and then use it to make prints of circular patterns.

❺ If available, use the base of a felled tree or a large log (the best size is that of a stepping stone) for children to paint the rings of the tree or their own circular pattern. Once dry, lay out these 'stepping stones' to walk along. If more easily available, painting on circular stones is also an interesting activity. Both of these activities present challenging tactile experiences.

❻ Find a piece of wallpaper or wrapping paper that features circles. Stick a small piece of it in the top left corner of a large sheet of paper and encourage the children to continue the pattern in paint (or other media).

❼ Children paint circles – large, small, overlapping, intersecting, inside other circles, etc. They can use different colours on large pieces of paper for maximum effect.
Extend the idea by making a collage, sticking on circular objects (e.g. buttons, discs of card, tissue paper circles, sequins).

❽ Encourage the children to experiment with writing ever larger circles in pencil or thin felt tip using the ideas template (page 41). They should try to start writing the circle at the one o'clock position but at this stage the emphasis is on 'feeling' the anticlockwise movement and on making a complete circle. (**NB:** this idea works well with squares and triangles too.)

❾ The drawings on the right provide further ideas for exploring circle patterns in any medium.

❿ Talk about the curly caterpillar letters that are written from an anticlockwise circular movement beginning: c, a, d, o, s, g, q, e, f. *Penpals: Foundation 2* deals with the teaching of these letters.

⑨ Make the monsters spotty.

Put the wheels on these vehicles.

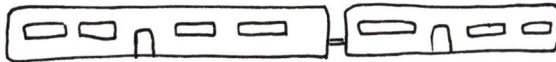

Trace the patterns.

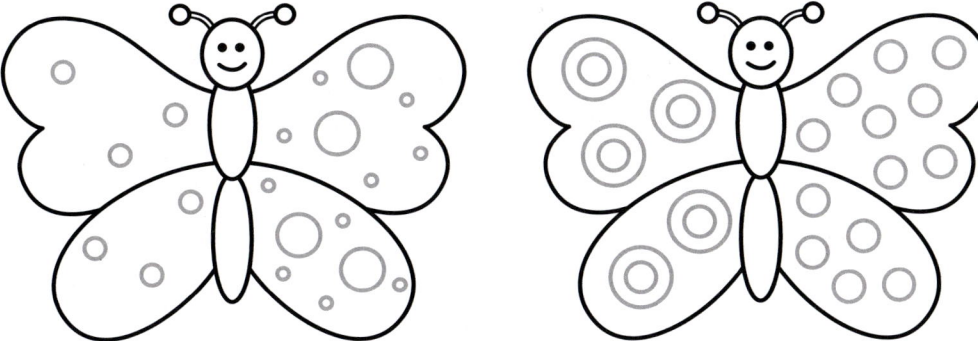

Make patterns on the butterflies.

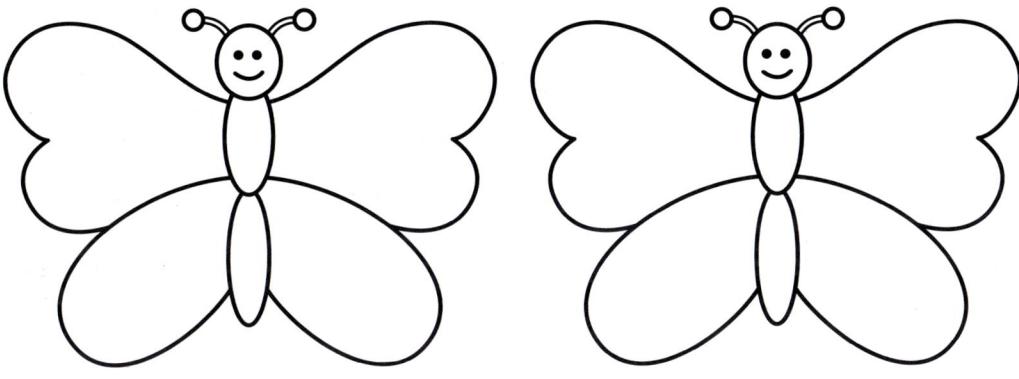

 **On the Penpals CD-ROM:
Investigating circles**

Warm up
- Gross and fine motor skills: Owl eyes

Talk about
- Draw children's attention to the circles in their environment whilst developing the vocabulary for describing them.
- Children can find patterns: Patterns inside and out, Looking up and down, Animal patterns.
- Talk about the curly caterpillar letters: c, a, d, o, s, g, q, e, f.

Try
- Chase
- Complete the shapes
- Ever increasing circles!

Penpals pad
- Encourage your children to make pictures containing circles – think of cars, buses, apples, faces, …

Gallery
- Add your own images of patterns your children have made – either as scans or digital photographs. You can even add images from the internet of patterns that you want to talk to the children about.

13 | Developing patterns and basic letter movements: investigating angled patterns

Early Learning Goal links: Handwriting plus Language for communication; Language for thinking; Writing; Shape, space and measures; Exploration and investigation; Movement; Using tools and materials; Exploring media and materials.

Ten ideas for investigating angled patterns

❶ Make cross-curricular links by talking about angled movements (sharp, jagged movements, for example) in PE, music, art and number work. Look for sharp angles in the environment – fences, road markings, branches in a tree, etc. Show the children that a vertical zig-zag often represents lightning.

❷ In PE, encourage children to make angled movements (e.g. walking stiffly like a robot but using bent limbs to exaggerate the angles) while moving along a zig-zag path. Sky writing zig-zags in the air or on each other's backs keeps the gross motor skill awareness at the forefront of the experience so that confidence is gained.

❸ Use the language of handwriting with the children so that they develop the oral skills to talk about pattern and feel confident enough to experiment. Talk about angled movements, diagonal lines, straight lines, jagged patterns and points.

❹ Working with thick paint, children try scratching angled patterns using forks, combs, hairpins, toothbrushes, etc.

❺ Children use wax to create angled patterns on paper. Then they wash over the paper with diluted paint to reveal the patterns that have been drawn.

❻ Children bend pipe cleaners into angled patterns and fix them together to make crazy towers. Use Plasticine as a base if the children want to make 3D models.

❼ Children paint triangles – large, small, overlapping, intersecting, inside other triangles. They can use different colours on large pieces of paper for maximum effect.

❽ Encourage the children to experiment with writing ever larger zig-zags and triangles. They should use a pencil or thin felt tip and keep going until they reach the edge of the paper, concentrating on keeping the angles sharp.

❾ Encourage the children to experiment with angled patterns using the ideas template (page 43).

❿ Talk about the zig-zag monster letters: v, w, x, z. *Penpals: Foundation 2* deals with the teaching of these letters. Many capital letters have angled patterns in them too: A, K, M, N, V, W, X, Y, Z.

Make more patterns.

Join the dots.

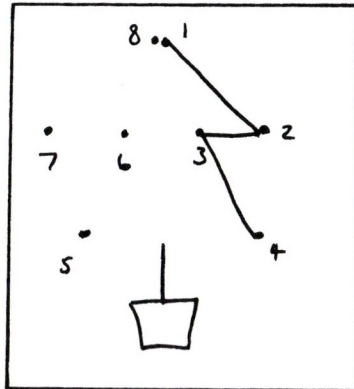

Give the crocodile some teeth.

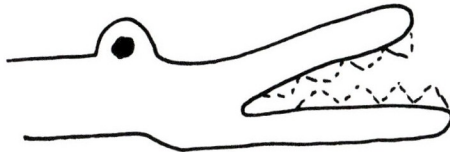

Trace the patterns.

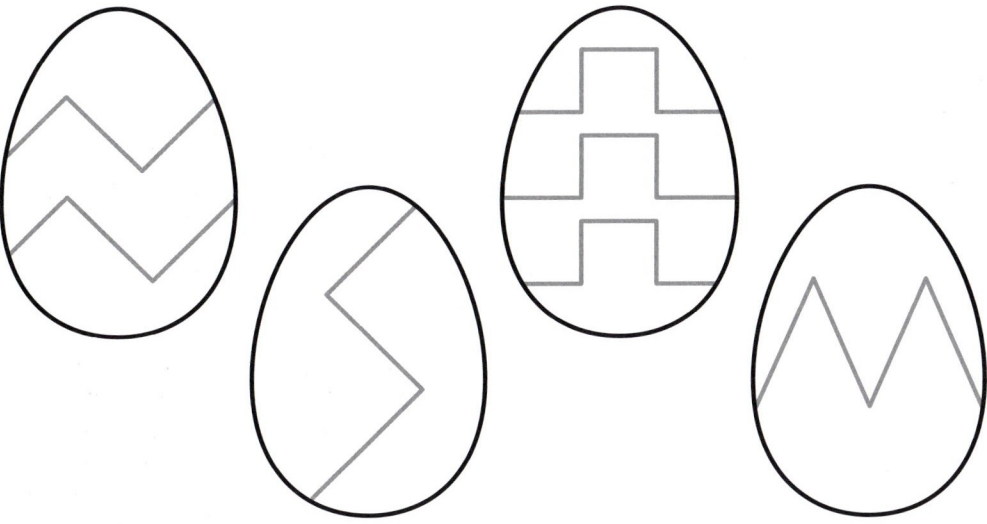

Make patterns in the eggs.

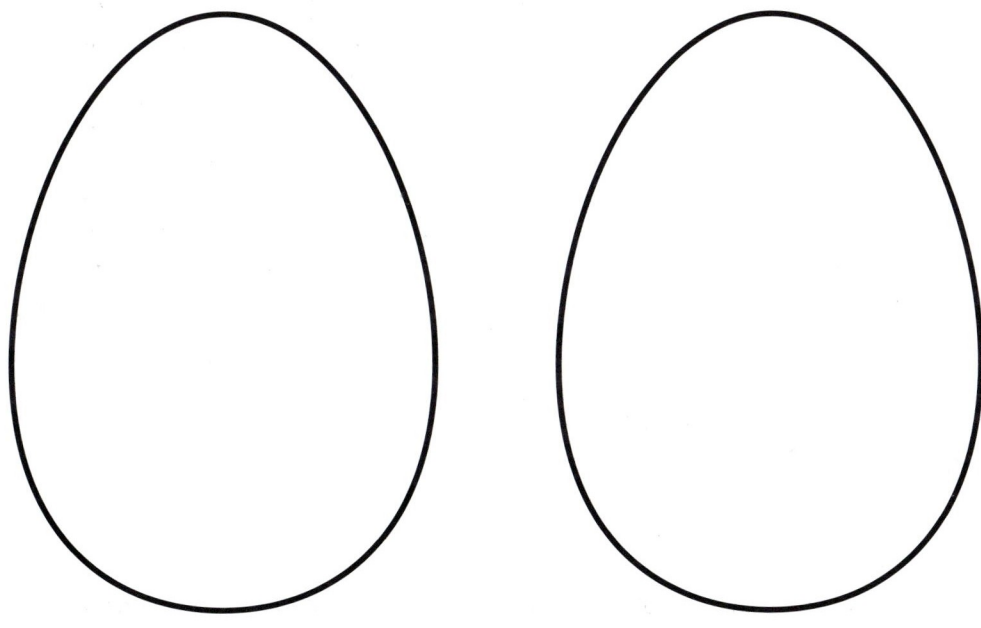

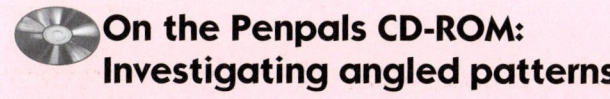

Early Learning Goal links: Handwriting plus Language for communication; Language for thinking; Writing; Shape, space and measures; Exploration and investigation; Movement; Using tools and materials; Exploring media and materials.

Ten ideas for investigating eights and spirals

NB: You may feel that these patterns are too demanding for very young children. They are, however, important patterns in the development of handwriting and encourage children to experiment with flow and direction. They also develop cross-lateral co-ordination. Give it a try and you may be surprised by the results!

❶ Make cross-curricular links by talking about eights and spirals in PE, music, art and number work. Look for these flowing patterns in the environment – fences, door numbers, shop logos, fabric design, etc. Show the children that a vertical eight is the same as a number 8.

❷ In PE, encourage children to make eight and spiral movements – running along a chalked pathway may help. Alternatively you could try using beanbags as a guiding path.
Sky writing eights or spirals in the air or writing these patterns on each other's back keeps the gross motor skill awareness at the forefront of the experience so that confidence is gained.

❸ Use the language of handwriting with the children so that they develop the oral skills to talk about pattern and feel confident enough to experiment. These patterns are particularly difficult so encourage the children to feel the pattern (with their eyes closed if necessary). Talk about circles, smooth flowing movements, crossing the line (which many children find very difficult to do initially), growing the spiral and shrinking the spiral.

❹ Working with thick paint, children use fingers to experiment with these patterns on table tops or thick card. They can try using both hands in turn and then together.

❺ Use a base board and four nails in a square shape. Allow the children to experiment with making eights using elastic bands.

❻ Children use skipping ropes to lay out eights or spirals. They can also bend pipe cleaners or play with wool to make eights and spirals.

❼ Children paint spirals – large, small, overlapping, starting in the middle, starting from the outside, working both clockwise and anticlockwise. They can use different colours on large pieces of paper for maximum effect.

❽ Encourage the children to trace over the spiral patterns in the left-hand section of the ideas template (page 45). They should trace the spirals both ways: from the inside out and from the outside in. They may like to use a different colour for each snail.

❾ Using pencil or thin felt tip, children experiment with growing and shrinking a spiral. Tricky but fun!

❿ Spirals and eights are linked to circles. Talk about the letters in the curly caterpillar family: c, a, d, o, s, g, q, e, f. Talk about the number 8 if appropriate.

① Make your shapes into pictures.

⑤

Trace the patterns.

Make spirals in the shells.

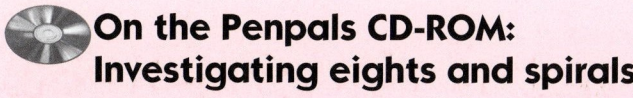

On the Penpals CD-ROM:
Investigating eights and spirals

Warm up
- Gross and fine motor skills: Falling seeds

Talk about
- Draw children's attention to the eights and spiral patterns in their environment whilst developing the vocabulary for describing them.
- Children can find patterns: Patterns inside, Patterns outside, Looking up, Looking down, Body patterns, Animal patterns.

Try
- Hit it, quick!
- Reveal the picture
- Finish the pattern

Penpals pad
- Let your children explore making eights and spirals on the screen.

Gallery
- Add your own images of patterns your children have made – either as scans or digital photographs. You can even add images from the internet of patterns that you want to talk to the children about.

Text of rhymes for hand and finger play

1a The Wheels on the Bus (*Track 11*)

The wheels on the bus go round and round,
Round and round,
Round and round,
The wheels on the bus go round and round,
All day long.

The wipers on the bus go swish, swish,
        swish, etc.

The people on the bus go chatter, chatter,
        chatter, etc.

Improvise other verses.

1b Grandmother's Glasses (*Track 12*)

These are Grandmother's glasses,
This is Grandmother's hat;
Grandmother claps her hands like this,
And rests them in her lap.

Repeat for Grandfather.

2a Peter Hammers (*Track 13*)

Peter hammers with one hammer, one hammer,
    one hammer,
Peter hammers with one hammer,
All day long.

Repeat for two, three, four and five hammers.

2b Heads, Shoulders, Knees and Toes (*Track 14*)

Heads, shoulders, knees and toes,
Knees and toes.
Heads, shoulders, knees and toes,
Knees and toes
And eyes and ears and mouth and nose,
Heads, shoulders, knees and toes,
Knees and toes.

3   Slowly, Slowly (*Track 15*)

Slowly, slowly, very slowly
Creeps the garden snail.
Slowly, slowly, very slowly
Up the wooden rail.
Quickly, quickly, very quickly
Runs the little mouse.
Quickly, quickly, very quickly
Round about the house.

4a Incy Wincy Spider (*Track 16*)

Incy Wincy Spider
Climbed up the water spout.
Down came the rain
And washed poor Incy out.
Out came the sunshine
and dried up all the rain,
So Incy Wincy Spider
Climbed up the spout again.

4b Here is the Church (*Track 17*)

Here is the church,
Here is the steeple,
Open the doors,
And here are the people.

5a Tommy Thumb (*Track 18*)

Tommy Thumb, Tommy Thumb,
Where are you?
Here I am, here I am,
How do you do!

Repeat for Peter Pointer, Finger Tall, Ruby Ring, Baby Small and Fingers All.

5b Five Little Peas (*Track 19*)

Five little peas in a peapod pressed,
One grew, two grew, and so did all the rest.
They grew … and they grew … and they
did not stop,
Until one day the pod went … POP!

6a Firework (*Track 20*)

Here is a sparkler.
Hold it with care.
Scribble with gold
In the cold night air.

Here are the flames
That flicker and burn.
See how they dance
As they twist and turn.

And here is the rocket
That races high.
See how it bursts
In the brilliant sky.

(© Tony Mitton, 1996)

6b In and Out the Dusty Bluebells (*Track 21*)

In and out the dusty bluebells,
In and out the dusty bluebells,
In and out the dusty bluebells,
Won't you be my partner?
Tippy tippy tap tap
On your shoulder,
Tippy tippy tap tap
On your shoulder,
Tippy tippy tap tap
On your shoulder,
Won't you be my partner?

7b Round and Round the Garden (*Track 22*)

Round and round the garden
Like a teddy bear,
One step,
Two steps,
Tickly under there.

8 Jack and Jill (*Track 23*)

Jack and Jill went up the hill
To fetch a pail of water.
Jack fell down and broke his crown
And Jill came tumbling after.

10 One Potato, Two Potato (*Track 24*)

One potato, two potato,
Three potato, four,
Five potato, six potato,
Seven potato, more!